Pauline Dingle

ISBN no. 10-55056-302-5

Canadian Cataloguing in Publication Data
Dingle, Pauline Ann, 1955-
   I'm dieting as fast as I can

   ISBN 1-55056-302-5
   1. Reducing diets. 2. Dieters. I. Title.
RM222.2.D56 1994   613.2'5   C9410458-2

Printed in Canada
Printed by Friesen Printers, Altona, Manitoba

Typesetting by David Blair, Abbotsford, B.C.
Cover production by Sandy Crawford of The Art Department, a division of Canada Wide Magazines Ltd., Burnaby, B.C.

Contents

Dedication

This book is dedicated to my husband Jon, and our children Ryan and Rebecca.

Do what you can
Be what you are
Shine like a glow worm
If you can not be a star.

Acknowledgments

With special thanks to:

Laura Dewar for her insight and inspiration;

Nomi Ahmed and Scott McLagen for their computer expertise and assistance;

Byron Johnson, of Friesen Printers for his patience and understanding; and

Peter Legge, President and Publisher of Canada Wide Magazines Ltd. for his support.

— ***Pauline Ann (Kurchak) Dingle***
  April 27, 1994

Chapter 1

I'm Dieting As Fast As I Can

I am not a doctor, a weight specialist, or a diet guru — but, I was a **diet junkie**.

You see, between the ages of ten and thirty, I was miserably unhappy with my body. And as a result, I tried everything and anything short of surgery to attain that perfectly slim, perfectly sculpted figure that continued to remain just perfectly beyond my grasp. And in my relentless pursuit of slenderness, I became *addicted* to dieting.

So desperate was I to be thinner, that any diet succeeded in wetting my emotional taste buds — spurring me on to yet another fruitless starvation regime. In fact, the weirder the diet, the more bizarrely appealing it became, as I frantically searched for the magical combination of foods that would "fix" my imperfect body forever. Oh, how I longed to be able to step proudly along the beach in a sexy bikini, or slip into a hip-hugging pair of jeans — and feel fatless. Oh, how I hoped and prayed, and worried and wished that my dieting dreams would come true!

Consequently, the dawn of each new shiny diet rose bright with hopeful promise for me. As my mind danced with visions of skinny sugar plums, my body was forced to eat to the beat of yet another rigid weight watching regime. In essence, I was dieting as fast as I could and exercising as fast as I could … and getting absolutely *nowhere*!!!

1

WITH ALL OF THE MILES I'VE RUN, LAPS I'VE SWUM, AND AEROBIC CLASSES I'VE ATTENDED

And then, thank goodness, something happened! ... I reached a point in my life where I became physically and emotionally exhausted from attempting every new diet that burst onto the tabloid scene (not to mention repeating the same old ones that had miraculously "worked" once!). I was tired of counting calories, tired of replacing french fries with naked salads, and tired of eating grapefruit and eggs until the sight of them made my stomach involuntarily heave!

I was also tired of believing in exercise as a means of attaining my lifelong desire — the possession of those perfectly contoured Playboy-like hips and derriere I do **not** have, *never* have had, and *never* will have. I mean, with all the miles I've run, laps I've swum, and aerobic classes I've attended, it's surprising I have any hips left at all! But I do!

Once I reached this point, I stopped playing Diet and Exercise Roulette with my mind, body and food. Once I reached this point, I found the key to my success. But how did I arrive there? And what has enabled me to continue living happily and thinly ever after? Furthermore, how can you do the same?

The answer lies within this book — and *yourself*!

I realize that everyone's weight problem is unique — the nature of yours may be very different from mine. You, for example, may be obese, and I never was. You may hate your stomach, whereas I hated my hips. You may think you are fat when you really are not. However, regardless of our different physical and mental spaces, the underlying problems that pervert our relationship with food are strikingly similar.

What follows is a culmination of experiences and perceptions involving myself and others that has guided me towards conquering my abnormal preoccupation with weight. I have found a way to stop the merry-go-round of dietitis and exercisitis that I painfully and unrealistically tortured myself with over the years. I have found a way to stop wasting a disproportionate amount of my precious time and energy, spinning in circles like a hamster in a cage in my futile quest to be thinner.

I do not claim to have all the answers — *no one* does! But, I do know this. Food is no longer an enemy to me now; and I am no longer its prisoner. After countless years of "battle," I am at peace with myself and my body.

And in the process … *I have **never** been this thin for this long in my entire life*! And I am confident that I will remain this way!

At last, I have overcome my obsession with weight. It is my hope that this book can do the same for you!

Chapter 2

Metabolism

I HATE MY SISTER-IN-LAW ANNE!

Well, I actually don't "hate" Anne. In fact, she is truly one of my favorite people and best friends, but I must confess I am extremely envious of her. You see, Anne is one of "those" people who can devour the top layer of a box of Turtles in one fell swoop! At family birthdays, it's Auntie Anne who has the corner piece of cake with the most roses — ***and then has seconds***! Anne also routinely devours two or three Jelly Donuts in the car on the way home from her weekly Thursday morning grocery shopping. (Grrr ... I get upset just thinking about it!)

"But what," you may query, "does Anne look like?" Well, Anne is a mother in her forties who has a perfectly proportioned figure. She is healthfully slim with shapely legs, slender hips, and a trim waistline. Anne is not a bona fide bonerack by any stretch of the imagination, but neither is she pleasantly plump nor noticeably bulging out in one specific area. In fact, Anne's only "problem spot" can be found at the tops of her arms — but then again, how many people have to struggle to pull designer jeans over their biceps, hold their breath while they zip up, and then live in agony for the rest of their confinement?!

Now, I don't want to give the impression that Anne is lazy, inactive, and undeserving of a cute figure. On the contrary, Anne is an extremely vivacious, athletic individual who bubbles over with enthusiasm and energy. However, the "fat" of the matter is this: I am just as active as Anne — if not more so! — but, I can not eat as much as she does without paying a hefty price (vis-à-vis those extra pounds and inches right around my hips and derriere!).

I guess what I envy most about Anne is that her life is not dominated by food, dieting, and the bathroom scale. Consequently, she is spared the relentless stream of worry over what she's eating, and where it will end up on her body. In retrospect, I can now see that I was unsuccessfully dieting and exercising as fast as I could, in hopes of achieving the physical and emotional state Anne enjoys naturally. A physical and emotional state that allows Anne the luxury of eating, without the tormenting guilt afterwards … or the anguishing task of trying to squeeze into a pair of pants that did fit perfectly well a few weeks ago!

When Anne does feel her clothes become a little snug, she says, "I never diet. Because then I constantly think about food and find myself eating way more than I normally would!" (Sound familiar?!)

So what does Anne do when she starts to feel heavier — say, after the Christmas holidays?

Well, she simply cuts down a little on her food consumption. And cutting down to Anne does not mean nibbling on salads without dressing, or consuming only proteins, or chomping on sackfuls of rabbit food. Cutting down to Anne simply means just having a little bit less of everything she normally eats. For example, instead of having two pieces of birthday cake, she will have only one — the corner piece covered with the most roses, of course!

FOOD FOR THOUGHT

The facts are plain and simple:
1) *Anne is thin, and*
2) *Anne doesn't diet, and*
3) *Anne never falls into the "fat trap" of worrying incessantly about her weight and what she eats.*

The question is why? A pervasive, unqualified why.

Let's begin by examining how dieters have more than food to contend with on their dieting plates. Something far more potent and much stronger than willpower alone!

VOLKSWAGENS AND PORSCHES

No two people have been, are, or ever will be identical in any "weigh," shape, or form! This is a given; a fact of life. And as such, we each come equipped with our very own physical plant that tirelessly and miraculously hums away behind the scenes to sustain our survival. And there is one facet of our physical plant — *metabolism* — that carries a great deal of significance as far as our weight is concerned.

Simply put, our *metabolism* is responsible for converting food into energy. And under its realm, there operates a key shaker and mover in the world of calorie counters and weight worriers. It is ... *metabolic rate.*

You see, your *metabolic rate* determines the rate of speed with which your body processes calories. And this, in turn, plays a leading role in establishing just how much you weigh in relation to how much you eat.

To put this in perspective, it helps to think of the body as a machine, an automobile for example ...

Human beings, like cars, need fuel to function. And just as various makes and models of cars have different bodies and fuel efficiencies; various "makes" and "models" of people have different body types and different *metabolic rates*.

Now a car's fuel efficiency determines how far that vehicle can travel on a tankful of gas. Likewise, an individual's metabolic rate determines just how far a person can "go" on a plateful of food.

In light of this, some of us are like the economical Volkswagen Beetle. Our bodies have energy efficient motors that doggedly churn out maximum mileage from each and every calorie. Consequently, we eat less but weigh more (much to our frustration and chagrin!), than lucky people like Anne whose gas-guzzling, racing car metabolisms require greater amounts of fuel.

Calorically speaking, this means that if Anne and I are together for an entire day performing *exactly* the same activities … Anne's body (with its speedy metabolic engine) may burn up 3,000 calories, whereas my body (the fuel efficient VW) may draw upon only 2,000!

Hold onto that concept (and the image of slim, beautiful Anne eating two pieces of Birthday Cake, three Jelly Donuts, and the top layer of a box of Turtles), while you contemplate this.

I WAS DOWNRIGHT MORTIFIED AT THE THOUGHT!

I'll never forget the day my girlfriend Laura nearly shocked the dieting daylights right out of me. As we were sitting and chatting over a cup of tea one afternoon (no sugar; a touch of skim milk for me), Laura questioned my eating and exercise habits. She was appalled by the fact that not only was I constantly dieting; but also after I ate, I felt compelled to go out and jog "it" off. Consequently, she was worried (and justifiably so!) about my physical and emotional well-being.

To throw added emphasis behind her concern, Laura described the plight of Debbie ... a co-worker who was having tremendous difficulty losing weight *on a diet of 900 calories a day*! ***Can you imagine***?! I most certainly could not! My initial reaction was one of scepticism over Debbie's dieting scruples. "No doubt about it!" I smugly thought to myself. "She obviously has to be cheating!"

However, Laura went on to explain that Debbie's diet was clinically supervised and Debbie was, in fact, being faithful to her weight loss program. Yet, despite her exhaustive efforts, she was pitted against her body in a perpetual tug-of-war to wrestle each and every recalcitrant pound away.

Needless to say, when I finally digested what Laura was saying, I was utterly mortified! ... I could hardly believe that under clinical supervision *and* the most stringent diet conditions, some unfortunate souls were stuck with bodies that stubbornly resisted relinquishing weight — even when spoon-fed a mere 900 calories a day!!

 FOOD FOR THOUGHT

How did these people feel? And what were they going to do? ... Live the rest of their lives on 800/700/600/___ calories a day?!

And what was I going to do? Live the rest of mine on the 1,200/1,100/1,000/___ daily calories it took to first ensure and then maintain my weight loss?!

While these disturbing thoughts raced through my mind, I quickly pushed them aside. Because at that point in my life, I despised my hips and bum so much I was still prepared to do almost anything to get rid of them. At that point in time, I was a desperate diet junkie whose hopeless addiction was fed by the unwavering belief that if I dieted long and hard enough, I would one day be permanently rewarded with the ultimate dieter's "high" — a perfect figure!

Thus, instead of thanking my lucky stars I did not have a metabolism like Debbie's; I continued to wish upon a star (and every diet under it!) that I could look like Anne and eat like Lynn — someone who makes Anne's food consumption seem like ... well, you be the judge!

IT SIMPLY ISN'T FAIR!

While I may envy Anne, my feelings toward Lynn can best be described as sheer, unadulterated jealousy! For string bean Lynn (or the Stick Lady as she is so aptly nicknamed) literally **never stops eating**! And by eating, I mean consuming (and thoroughly enjoying!) all of those outlawed No-No foods we less fortunate "fatties" drool over in our sleep ... Hot Fudge Brownie Delights, Double Deluxe Pizzas, and Mushroom Bacon Cheeseburgers with fries!

And do you think that skinny Lynn has ever thought twice about a calorie or carbohydrate? Not in her life! No diet pop, diet ice cream, or diet anything has ever graced that girl's thin lips. In fact, I doubt she even knows the meaning of the word NutraSweet!

 FOOD FOR THOUGHT

Can you imagine being able to eat exactly what you want, when you want, and in the amounts you want ... and be thin?!

"It isn't fair!" my mind protests as I enviously watch Lynn return from her *second* trip to the buffet table with *another* heaping plateful.

"It isn't fair!" my mind reiterates as I stare stupefied while she tucks into *another* piece of Amaretto Cheesecake! "It isn't fair! It simply *is not* fair!!"

A CASE OF CERTIFIABLE DISCRIMINATION

The vast discrepancies between how much people weigh in relation to how much they eat, coupled with the overwhelming number of dieting failures, prompted me to question, "**Why**?!" Regardless of what the experts advocated, the mounting evidence began to outweigh the validity of certain dieting truths for me. I simply knew too many people who ate a lot and were thin (like Anne and Lynn) ... and too many who didn't eat much and weren't (Debbie and myself included)!

In essence, my personal experiences and perceptions became too potent, too blatantly convincing to be denied! ... Eventually leading me to the realization that being fat or thin sometimes has nothing at all to do with how "good" or "bad" we are with food. Or the amount of willpower any of us exerts. Or how much or little we eat. The unfair fat of the matter, is that some lucky individuals are able to eat considerably more than others and remain substantially thinner, because *every "body's" metabolism functions at a different metabolic rate*!

I mean, bonerack Lynn is one of the skinniest (the *very* skinniest) people I have ever met in my entire life and she eats the very most! This is a clear-cut case of certifiable discrimination. *and* ... there isn't a damn thing that you, or I, or anyone else can do about it!

With that in mind, I'd like you to temporarily rein in your weight watching horses. Because as we continue our journey, we will come across other circumstances that are likely to challenge your belief system as far as food and weight and dieting are concerned. And these encounters may provoke feelings of disbelief and discomfort. If so, don't be alarmed ... those feelings are perfectly natural. You see, this book involves *a process*. One that takes time to absorb and accept. Therefore, when and if you experience a flicker of doubt or denial along the way, just stop and ask yourself this.

FOOD FOR THOUGHT

If your past diets had been successful — wouldn't you be thin and happy right now?!

Hold onto that thought as you embrace the ideas to come. You have nothing to lose, and everything to gain (literally, and not figuratively, so-to-speak!).

THE MAGICAL REALM

It is a scientific "fact" that a person must consume an extra 3,500 calories in order to gain one pound. Likewise, they must intake 3,500 less in order to shed that pound. I say *balderdash!* While this may be true for some, *it is not the golden rule for all!*

Need some concrete proof? Let's head down south and then to a maternity ward!

MARGARITAVILLE

In the summer of 1979, I spent three weeks vacationing in Mexico with Anne and Lucy, two of my husband's sisters. Now the first ten days of our holiday we resided in Mexico City, where every morning I "indulged" in half a cantaloupe filled with cottage cheese in lieu of the full American breakfasts enjoyed by my skinnier familial companions! In contrast, during the last half of our sojourn, we inhabited a small untouristed town by the sea where edible food as we know it was virtually non-existent. For example, when searching for something to eat in the local marketplace one morning, we were aghast after glimpsing the hanging corpse of a fly-encrusted chicken ... at least we thought it was a chicken! (Are you starting to get the picture?!)

Furthermore, of the three of us, just who do you think was determined (and stupid!) enough to jog daily in the altitude and pollution of Mexico City, *and then* in the sauna-like heat and humidity of the coast?! Moi, of course! As for Anne and Lucy? Ho hum, they burned up their calories suntanning and exercising their eyeballs reading by the pool!

So, how did each of us fair weightwise upon our arrival home?

Well … Anne, the sister-in-law who always eats the corner piece of birthday cake with the most roses and then has seconds, *lost* five pounds. Lucy, the sister-in-law who slaved for a year to lose weight after having a baby (more on that to follow), *remained the same*. And I, naturally, *gained* six and a half pounds!?

 FOOD FOR THOUGHT

And 3500 calories are supposed to equal one pound for every "body?!"

Fat chance!

SHE LEFT THE MATERNITY WARD IN HER SIZE NINE DESIGNER JEANS!

Erica has an eating reputation just like Lynn, the Stick Lady! At get-togethers it's pencil thin Erica whose plate is **always** piled higher and deeper than everyone else's — *including the men!* Thus, Erica is the brunt of much ribbing and many a joke. Does this bother her? Are you kidding! She just shrugs her shoulders and chuckles good-naturedly as she digs into her food with care-free abandon. You see, Erica has the last laugh … her figure is model thin, *and* she eats exactly what her little old stomach desires without one iota of mental indigestion!

I guess the very best way to convey Erica's natural ability to be thin is to recount the time she was pregnant. Erica gained forty-three pounds with with her son Justin, but left the maternity ward *in her size nine designer jeans*! Can you believe it? … Some women struggle for months to shed weight after childbirth. Take my sister-in-law Lucy (of Margaritaville "fame") who gained only nineteen pounds during her pregnancy — *but*, was forced to fight with the might of a sumo wrestler for an entire year before she was finally able to get rid of it!

 FOOD FOR THOUGHT

When you compare Erica and Lucy's postpregnancy weight loss in simple mathematical terms, it doesn't make sense! Because Erica gained twice as much as Lucy. But … it took Lucy seventy-five times longer, plus months of conscientious dieting and exercising to eventually lose hers! And some mothers (bless their poor cellulite!) never manage to recapture their original figures.

Contrast these women to Erica.

It doesn't take a rocket scientist to calculate that the numerical figures (not to mention the physical ones!) just don't add up. There's definitely something wrong with this equation!

I'll tell you what's wrong! …

3500 calories **do not** *always equal one pound for* **every** *"body!"*

Why?

Because every "body" has a different metabolic rate.

CINDY LOOKED HEAVIER NOW THAN I HAD EVER SEEN HER!

Upon arriving at a dinner party one evening, I was instantly mortified by the sight of Cindy, a friend and colleague. My stomach cartwheeled as my mind reeled in shock waves. Why? Because from the previous November to May, Cindy had ever so slowly lost thirty-seven and a half pounds by eating salads, chicken, fish, plain yogurt and unbuttered popcorn. Oh yes, there was one other key ingredient to her weight loss program — diet pills!

And just how were Cindy's months of monk-like deprivation rewarded?

Well, a mere twelve weeks earlier, a much slimmer and trimmer Cindy boarded a plane to return to the States for the summer holidays. But now it was early fall. And there she sat before me, terribly self-conscious and visibly uncomfortable in a body that had all too quickly mushroomed back up to its original size, and then some!

As my mind struggled to digest the situation, my memory instinctively flashed back to the previous winter. During that time, Cindy and I had engaged in many lengthy discussions, vigorously contemplating the ups and downs of dieting. In particular, our conversations revolved around her painfully slow weight loss, which frustrated her to no end *because she was not cheating*!

Having been that route countless times before, I could poignantly relate to Cindy's dieting distress and understood perfectly well her perturbed frustration. Consequently, I tried to be as supportive and encouraging as possible — even extending an open invitation for her to contact me whenever she felt the urge to pig out, quit altogether, or simply talk. (Note: At that point in my life, I still believed in diets and was maintaining my skinny weight by existing primarily on tinned tuna … water-packed, of course!)

But after Cindy had "failed," and failed so miserably — by not only regaining the weight, *but also regaining it so very quickly!* — what comfort could I possibly be to her? I mean, what could I say or do that would cushion her injured pride and help rebuild her shattered self-esteem?

 FOOD FOR THOUGHT

Trying to lose weight is inexplicably exasperating and downright depressing! At times, it seems dieters have a greater chance of being struck by lightning than shedding just one measly pound! However, even more demoralizing is when we bravely endure the physical and emotional torture of dieting — only to put the weight right back on again!!

What a devastating blow to our psyches!

All of that self-denial and the associated stress that goes along with it, and *for what*?

For a fleeting moment of success that abruptly crashes when the weight begins to skyrocket and we find ourselves plummeting into the stark, humiliating self-actualization of fatness and failure?

It's like taking a roller coaster ride.

Climbing that first and steepest incline parallels the tedious pound by pound, week by week weight loss. Reaching the crest of the hill represents that ever so brief moment of happiness when the desired weight has been attained and we are on top of the world! And then ... the split second downhill plunge seems like all the time it takes to collectively wipe out every single agonizing moment of deprivation. And there we are, psychologically battered, physically fatter, and desperate to scramble back onto that precarious diet coaster — *again*!?!

And for what?!

The answer is for nothing ... *absolutely nothing!*

Because in spite of Cindy's Herculean efforts, she looked heavier at that dinner party than I had ever seen her before! And since then, her dieting attempts have been equally ill-fated and disastrous, following this predictable pattern.

Cindy diets and ever so slowly loses weight. But then she balloons up immediately thereafter (often surpassing her prediet starting point)! So she embarks upon yet another diet, painstakingly reshedding the pounds — only to find herself fat again virtually overnight. And up and down. And down and up the weight yo-yos.

And the mere thought of it all makes me want to throw up! Because I have been where Cindy is at. In fact, I spent over twenty years of my life seesawing from one weight (and diet) to another ... until I *finally* came to the realization that, like Cindy, I was a classic victim of the *yo-yo syndrome*. A textbook case who had fallen prey to its rebounding rhythm. Come follow the bouncing weight with me. I think you will find the tune surprisingly familiar!

THE YO-YO SYNDROME

In retrospect, when I was firmly hooked to the end of that dieting string, my body would predictably yo-yo up and down between two clearly established points on the scale — my *top* and *bottom weights.*

Starting at my *bottom weight.*

In order to be my very skinniest, I had to eat like Gandhi and exercise like an Olympic athlete. I honestly don't think I could be any thinner unless I was stricken with a deadly disease! (Is this not true for you, too? I mean, don't you have to subject yourself to concentration camp-like eating conditions in order to be your "skinniest?" And didn't Cindy have to do the same?)

Climbing up the scale …

Once I stopped dieting, I *always* gained weight! And with that inevitable weight gain, the needle on the scale seemed to soar instinctively to rest at my *set weight* — a weight midway between my *bottom* and *top weights*; a weight where my body seemed to feel the most comfortable.

And upon arriving at my *set weight,* one of two things would happen. Usually, I would remain firmly positioned at that familiar niche. However, at other times, I would land there temporarily … and then continue to put on the pounds until I tipped the scales at the very heaviest I have ever been — my *top weight.*

Now my *top weight* seemed to be as far as my body was naturally willing to stretch, resisting being any heavier *unless* I was to blatantly overeat … which I never did. Because once I reached that weight, I'd panic and go on another diet! Consequently, my *top weight* did not progressively spiral upward. In fact, it has remained the same since I was fourteen years old — again, because whenever I hit that number on the scale I would *immediately* diet.

Unfortunately, however, many chronic dieters (like Cindy) find themselves ballooning up higher and higher after each diet, leapfrogging past their previous *top weight* to become even heavier than they were to begin with!

Why?

 FOOD FOR THOUGHT

Why is it that dieters have to work so very hard to lose weight … and then having done so, promptly put it back on?!

Furthermore…

Why do so many dieters gain even more weight than they originally lost?!

The answer, in many cases, is a simple matter of cause and effect. After the deprivation of dieting, people overeat ... and when you overeat, you gain weight. As Sharon puts it, "Once I stop dieting, I go after all of those foods I wasn't allowed to have and attack them with a vengeance!"

But ...

 FURTHER FOOD FOR THOUGHT

While there is no doubt that overeating is a major reason for weight gain (postdiet or not!), it is not (I repeat not!) the only reason.

How can I be so sure?

Read on!

I WAS COMPLETELY INNOCENT OF ANY MASSIVE OVEREATING VIOLATION!

When going home for the summer after teaching abroad for the year (and after dieting voraciously in anticipation of the event), I would always be in a state of panic as to what clothes to pack. My husband Jon could never understand why deciding what to take was such a major production for me.

"Just throw a few things in a suitcase," he'd say matter-of-factly (as only a man without a weight problem could!).

And as I started to protest the impossibility of that simple suggestion, an enticing wave of expectancy pulsated throughout my psyche. "Maybe (just maybe!) this time will be different!" I joyfully speculated. "Maybe (just *maybe*!) I won't gain weight!"

But, I was wrong! My naive hopefulness was repeatedly short-lived. For I would arrive home thin ... and leave at the end of the summer being fat (ten to fifteen pounds primarily ring-around-the-hips fatter!). In fact, I can distinctly remember June

18

of 1985 when I gained *seven* pounds after being home for just *eleven* days!

Can you believe it?!

I most certainly could not. Because in my case, the perplexing and unfair "fat" of the matter was this.

With all other possible reasons aside (water retention, jet lag, menstrual weight gain, etc.), I **know** — in fact, I'd *swear* on a stack of bibles! — that in the space of those *eleven* days, I did **not** consume anywhere in the neighbourhood of the 24,500 calories needed to put on *seven* extra pounds. I was completely innocent of any massive overeating violation!

And how about Cindy, who regained her "lost" thirty-seven and a half pounds in less than twelve weeks. Did she intake the equivalent of *one hundred and thirty one thousand* calories above and beyond her body's basic requirements during that period of time?!

I doubt it!

 FOOD FOR THOUGHT

If I hadn't consumed the number of calories that technically substantiated my weight gain, and if others haven't either — what happens?

Well, I see it this way …

DIETING YOURSELF INTO FATNESS

After years of subjecting myself to wave after wave of futile deprivation, it *finally* dawned on me that repetitive dieting wreaks havoc upon our metabolic systems. So much so, that the honourable intentions and convictions of dieters can actually backfire on them over a period of time! To understand how this happens, let's take a look at dieting from the body's perspective.

To begin with, a body is incapable of distinguishing between true famine and that which is self-imposed (dieting). Therefore, it interprets every prolonged food shortage as life threatening ... and responds by becoming more energy efficient and functioning at a slower metabolic rate. And this is where a dieter's problems originate and then escalate!

For in reality, the faster a metabolic rate, the more quickly calories are burned and the thinner a person will be! But constant dieting forces a metabolism to burn calories more slowly and become exceedingly adept at getting by on less — thereby inhibiting rather than promoting weight loss.

Moreover, from the moment we arbitrarily decide to end a diet, our minds switch immediately from starvation mode, but our metabolisms do not. Oh no. Our diet battered metabolisms (stung by the fear and instability generated by past "famines") continue to operate ultraefficiently; simultaneously grasping every opportunity to reclaim the lost weight and stockpile any extra ... until absolutely certain that *the famine (or threat thereof) is really and truly over!*

In the meantime (much to our horror and dismay!), the pounds quickly return to haunt us, even though we are *not* overeating and the number of calories consumed *do not* account for the number of pounds gained given the "3500-calories-to-one-pound" ratio!

So how does this make us feel? Why, angry, fat and miserable! So what do we do? Panic and go on another diet. Only to lose the weight and then pack it all on again. Which forces us back to square one — again. And again and again. Because the longer, greater and more frequent the food deprivation, the further our metabolisms are driven to function upon less and conserve more. And this, when taken to the extreme, leads to the worst case metabolic scenario — "dieting ourselves into fatness" — where we end up in the frustrating and perplexing position *of having to diet in order not to gain weight,* as opposed to dieting to lose it!!

20

FOOD FOR THOUGHT

Those of us who believe we are doing ourselves a favour by continually dieting to become thinner, may unwittingly be accomplishing the opposite!

Ironically, the metabolic hari-kari spawned by the feast and famine of cyclical dieting can leave us heavier than ever and susceptible to gaining weight very, very easily ... while eating less than ever before!

Our bodies deserve far more credit for striving to ensure our survival than we would like, given our unrelenting desire to be thinner, don't they?

Here's another example of that metabolic defence mechanism in action.

THE PLATEAU

Haven't we all dieted merrily along our weight watching way, only to come face to face with the dreaded *plateau*? There it sits smack dab in the middle of our dieting path ... that infuriating period of time when the weight defiantly refuses to budge from its entrenched position *regardless* of how "good" we have been.

Why?

FOOD FOR THOUGHT

Why is it that a dieted body reaches a point where, based upon reduced caloric consumption, weight should have been lost, but isn't?

I mean using simple mathematics, when a person intakes 3500 fewer calories, there should be a subsequent one pound weight loss, right?

Wrong!

As many of us have experienced firsthand, that's not always the case. Here's why.

When faced with yet another "famine," a dieted body valiantly struggles to cling onto its existing weight by becoming even more energy efficient. But ... a metabolism can only hold the fort and push itself to function upon so little for so long. Therefore, it eventually has no option but to draw upon its stored fat and release weight. And it is then (if we have persevered), that we finally see the anticipated results on the scale.

Now let's take a look at what transpires when a metabolism is forced to cope with the opposite situation — too much food!

FROM FAMINE TO FEAST

I can ashamedly remember occasions (usually sparked by mid-diet deprivation!) where I have literally attacked a whole bowl of nuts within seconds. Crazed with desire, hunger and guilt, I have frantically thrown handful after handful of those calorie-infested nuggets into my mouth as if I would never see another walnut, cashew or peanut again for as long as I lived! Hysterically promising myself all the while, "This is the last mouthful, the very last one!" ... Only to find my hand reaching compulsively for yet another!

 FOOD FOR THOUGHT

Haven't we all gone overboard with food?

And when we do, when we bombard our metabolism with a deluge of excess calories, just how is it supposed to handle the overflow? I mean, when you think about it, what is a metabolism to do when completely snowed under by an avalanche of food it doesn't need, but must digest?

Well, our metabolisms can effectively process extra food **up to a point** and **within reason**. That's because *metabolic rates* have the capacity to compensate for occasional moderate over-indulgences, but not larger, repeated ones. This means that most people can get away with minor caloric indiscretions, but pay a hefty price weightwise for excessive binging and perpetual overeating.

But ... just as we all have different metabolic rates, so we each have different metabolic capacities to process excess calories. And unfortunately, this is where well-intentioned "diet"hards unknowingly place themselves at a distinct disadvantage! Because habitual dieting handicaps a body's natural ability to process a normal number of calories — let alone compensate for larger doses. As a result ...

If Anne (a non-dieter) and I (a perpetual dieter) each consume 500 calories above and beyond our individual daily requirements (say we both have a corner piece of birthday cake with roses!) ... Anne's speedy, undieted racing car metabolism will likely burn off every single one of those additional calories; whereas my diet wracked body (with its ultraefficient, famine fearful Volkswagen engine) will not!

Oh no, my metabolism (haunted by memories of reoccurring starvation!) will quickly seize the excess and store it away for a calorie deficient day. Hence, I am the one who is left holding the fat! And before I know it, my body has succeeded in gathering enough to replenish that lost during dieting; and then some for added measure!

 FOOD FOR THOUGHT

Is this fair?

Of course not!

Is it a fact of life?

Yes!

When we refuse to accept our metabolisms for what they are and force them to become even more efficient through cyclical dieting.

READJUSTING YOUR METABOLIC RATE

Some people believe that *metabolic rates* can be adjusted to facilitate speedier weight loss by ... eating only certain foods or a combination of foods. Eating at specific times of the day. "Grazing" (eating small amounts frequently). Exercising before a meal as opposed to after. And so on and so forth.

Now while these methods may be met with some success, you *must* bear this in mind ...

What is really important with respect to weight loss and metabolic rates, is not how fast you lose the weight, but how long you keep it off. Because in reality, *the longer a person maintains a weight loss, the greater likelihood that individual has of maintaining it for good!*

For it is only after weight is kept off *for a period of time*, that a *metabolic rate* naturally readjusts and a lower *set weight* can be established. And both of these factors enable a recovering dieter to eat more (and more normally) without gaining weight. (This process took about eight months for me; but the time frame varies with individual metabolisms and dieting histories.)

Consequently, when I stopped ricocheting from one diet (and weight!) to another, my body gradually stabilized at a lower *set weight all on its own*! My fluctuation was replaced by stabilization.

Why?

Because my metabolism was no longer in a perpetual state of dithering turmoil and uncertainty over the amount of food and nutritives it would be given to work with from one day to the next!

In essence, my body became convinced (beyond a shadow of an excess calorie!) that *the famine*, and threat thereof, *was really and truly over*!!

 FINAL FOOD FOR THOUGHT ON METABOLISM

Each and every one of us knows an "Anne," a "Lynn" or "Erica" — people who have virtual carte blanche when it comes to what, when and how much they eat. And then there are others like Cindy who continue to diet, only to repeatedly regain the weight and feel like fat, frustrated failures. Not to mention Debbie who legitimately weight watches under clinical supervision only to discover her body can actually sustain itself on a meagre handful of calories a day!

What can we learn about weight and dieting from these people and their situations?

Plenty!

To begin with ... *3500 calories do not equal one pound for every "body!"*

In other words, a calorie is not a calorie, is not a calorie. Because three people with identical activity levels can eat **exactly** the same food, in **exactly** the same amounts, at **exactly** the same times of day, for **exactly** the same length of time ... **and**, one person will lose weight. Another will stay the same. And unfortunately, the third poor soul will gain! Why?

Because ... *every **"body"** has a different metabolic rate*!

And whether this is fair or not; whether we like it or not, we have to **accept** our metabolisms for what they are and who that makes us bodywise.

And within that physical and mental framework, we also have to *understand* this.

Repetitive dieting can actually undermine our honest attempts to lose weight by forcing our bodies to become more energy efficient and function at a slower metabolic rate ... until they perceive ***the famine (and any threat thereof) is truly over***! In the meantime, our famine sensitive systems simultaneously seize every opportunity to reclaim and stockpile as much weight as possible as protection against further deprivation. Thus (much to our frustration and chagrin!), when we stop dieting and start eating more than our bodies have been conditioned to receiving, we gain unsubstantiated weight.

And if that's not infuriating and demoralizing enough, we are often left with something far more unpalatable to stomach on our dieting plates ...

When taken to the extreme, chronic dieting creates the ultimate metabolic hari-kari. It holds the body hostage by virtually putting a gun to our metabolism's head and demanding it become increasingly efficient or face death by starvation! ... Placing us in the ironic and perplexing predicament *of having to diet in order **not** to gain weight*, as opposed to dieting to lose it!!

In a way, we are masters of our own metabolic destiny, aren't we? I mean, why can't we stop interfering with our bodies, eat normally, and allow our metabolisms to function the way God made them!

Chapter 3

Body Stamp

EVER SINCE I WAS TEN YEARS OLD

Over the past twenty years of my life, before I came to terms with food, I was guilty of playing a dangerous "losing" game with the natural functioning and weight of a healthy body. My father is Ukrainian, and so along with my high cheek bones and ability to tan well, I have been genetically endowed with Slavic hips. Instead of accepting those hips as a part of myself, I have been trying to "do something" about them since the age of ten. I can vividly recall my first encounter of the weight kind.

It was the middle of fifth grade. My parents had just bought a winter raincoat for me, and I was modelling it for my mom and aunt. As I faced them, both commented on how pretty the coat looked, but as I drew the front together and turned sideways, they both giggled. When I asked them what was so funny, my mom said kindly, "Nothing, dear — it's just with the way you were standing, your bum stuck out a little. That's all."

This incident, coupled with my uncle Peter's annoyance at the number of Black Magic Chocolates I ate at his house that Christmas, prompted me to embark upon my first diet. And from that day forward, the obsession began. I can't remember the name of my inaugural diet (I have been on too many since), but I do remember beginning the daily ritual of stepping ever so gingerly onto the scales, and peering down cautiously and expectantly to see where the weight of that black needle would lie.

Until recently, that needle was symbolic of my addictive struggle to be thinner. Until recently, that slender black needle ruled my life and happiness as I desperately attempted to defy my body stamp by fighting blindly and fiercely against it.

STEPPING EMOTIONALLY BEYOND MY HIPS AND DERRIERE

In retrospect, I now realize that my bodily unhappiness was fueled by the fact that I did not measure up (or more accurately, "down") to the current societal norm of physical perfection, ultraslimness. As a result, I was perpetually dissatisfied with my body, and perpetually placing myself under pressure to attain that long lean-legged, hipless look I was not born with!

It wasn't until I began living in Southeast Asia, that I started to see the size and shape of my body in a different light. It was during my three years in Thailand, that I began to step emotionally beyond my hips and derriere to become a willing participant in the process of accepting them. It was then I came to understand this …

Genetics plays a powerful role in determining body build and weight distribution.

With that in mind, let's size up the Thais.

NO MIRACLE DIETS, OR NUTRASWEET, OR JANE FONDA WORKOUTS KEEP THESE PEOPLE THIN!

Have you ever noticed how tiny and slender Oriental people are? The women are so delicate in stature they almost appear doll-like!

Well, the years I spent living in Bangkok certainly drove home that fact. For no matter how you look at it, the Thai people are an extremely petite race. So petite, I felt as big as a lumbering elephant amidst those diminutive, sylphlike females. So petite, that it is next to impossible for foreign men to find a department store that carries pants their size — if they have a waistline that exceeds 36 inches!

Now I am not insinuating that all Thais are slender. Of course, there are those who are fat and obese. But, heavy Thais are definitely the exception rather than the rule. Without a doubt, the vast majority are blatantly slim, tiny and small-boned!

And what I find absolutely mind-boggling about these thin people is that they are constantly *eating*. I mean, anyone would think *eating* was the Thai national pastime! For wherever you look, noodle carts, food stalls, and restaurants are crammed onto every corner and into every imaginable nook and cranny. And each one is filled to capacity with people — eating!

Furthermore, I did not witness hordes of sweat-soaked jogging enthusiasts fanatically running themselves ragged in Thailand (a common sight in North America). Nor did I spy masses of Danskinned "diet"hards pounding their way to thindom (and shin splints) through relentless aerobic workouts!

In all fairness, I must admit that the sweltering heat and humidity of Bangkok, plus the horrendous pollution and traffic, play a decisive role in stifling extracurricular physical activity. In addition, there is the economic reality. Most Thais are dancing as fast as they can to earn a living; not to lose weight. However, with economic and environmental factors aside, it is obvious that the slender Thai people do not exercise as much (or as obsessively!) as us "go for the burn" westerners!

 FOOD FOR THOUGHT

Thailand is a nation of thin, petite people who neither exercise profusely nor diet excessively. Why then, are the Thais — who are constantly eating! — so slim?

The answer lies within their genes. No miracle diets, or NutraSweet, or Jane Fonda Workouts keep these people thin — *they were simply born that way!*

Here's another example of that genetic fait accompli.

I KNOW WHAT MY MOTHER LOOKED LIKE AT FIFTY!

It was 110 scorching degrees as I left school one afternoon. While walking towards the parking lot, I looked up and noticed a movement on the playing field and thought to myself, "Who in their right mind is out there in this unmerciful heat?" Squinting and straining to ascertain the identity of the undulating figure, I realized it was Linda — *jogging!*

Now when I discovered who it was, it didn't surprise me. You see, Linda hates her figure and is always exercising and dieting to try and change it. But unfortunately, she always looks the same, pear-shaped.

Why?

Deep down Linda knows why. It was evident when she confided, "I'm frightened, Pauline. Because I know what my mother looked like at fifty, and I *shudder to think that one day I might look like her!*"

It was all I could do to refrain myself from retorting, "Hold on tight to your diet books and Nikes, Linda, because unfortunately, *you already do!!*"

SHE COULD DIET UNTIL HER DYING DAY AND RUN RINGS AROUND THE MOON

Linda is a physical carbon copy of her mother and her grandmother and great grandmother. In fact, all of the Clancey women are virtual mirror images of one another. Same smile, same eyes, same nose and ... same basic body shape. The fat of the matter is that each generation of females on Linda's mother's side of the family carries the bulk of their weight below their waists.

So what does that tell us?

It tells us that no amount of dieting or exercising is going to significantly alter Linda's pear shape. She could run rings around the moon and diet until her dying day, but … she will never succeed in dramatically overhauling the way her body has been put together. Why?

Because Linda can not change her genetically predetermined body stamp, *including where her weight is distributed on her body*. No one can.

I should know.

You see, for the longest time I refused to accept I was incapable of changing something that to a large extent was beyond my physical and emotional control. Just as Linda's pear shape and a Thai's petite body are biologically programmed, so my "big" childbearing hips were bequeathed to me by my genetic code. *But*, as simple and as rational as that may sound, I had tremendous difficulty getting that through my thick head.

My comprehension was clouded by the fact that throughout my life, hard work, perseverance and discipline had enabled me to accomplish my goals. Thus, I was at a loss to understand why those personality traits would not help me acquire the thin hips I desperately desired. For the life of me, I could not fathom that I was incapable of dieting, swimming, running, or doggie kicking my derriere away!

And to compound my frustration, I also had to contend with this.

Just as we can not dictate where our fat hangs its hat upon our body, we also have no control over where we lose weight. Take Linda, for example. Even if she lost a substantial amount of weight, there is absolutely no guarantee that the majority of those pounds would fall from the heaviest, pear-shaped part of her body.

Ironically (and unfortunately!), the areas where we wish to lose weight the most, are usually the last to relinquish their fat and the first to reclaim it!

I am a classic case of this twist of fatted fate. For whenever I gain weight, it *never* settles on my slim arms, skinny wrists or bony ankles. Oh no, it heads straight for them thar hips! And yet when I lose a few pounds, do you think those hips willingly release their excess? No way! They stubbornly hang onto each and every ounce of it for dear life!

Thus, after years of struggling with this exasperating phenomenon, I finally came to the following realization ...

MY BATHING SUIT BOTTOMS WILL ALWAYS CRAWL UP MY BUM!

Regardless of how thin I become (I could literally diet and exercise myself into a bag of bones!), my bum will always be bigger in relation to the rest of my body. Likewise, Linda will always have a pear shape; and others (like my girlfriend Julia) will never have perfectly flat stomachs — no matter how faithfully we count our calories and perform our bum rumbas and sit ups!

So what are we to do?

Throw up our hands in exasperated defeat and say, "To hell with watching our food intake!" and "Down with exercise!"

I mean, why bother if the genetic cards are so heavily stacked against us. Right?

Wrong!

Because each of us should strive to be the very best we can be. And in order to do so, we need to care about what we eat and how much we exercise. But in conjunction with that, we also need to step back and realistically assess our bodies and objectively identify what we can and can not change to improve our appearance.

And in the process, we *must* understand this …

There is an important distinction to be made between accepting the shape of our body versus accepting its size!

How? Why?

Read on!

BEING THE BEST YOU CAN BE

You are born with genes that stamp out your basic body type and where your fat will be distributed upon your body. However, this does not necessarily mean that if your mother is fat, and your grandmother is fat, that you are automatically doomed to be fat, too. Because you may have little control over the shape of your body, but you do have some control over the relative *size* of your shape — how big your waistline becomes; how wide your hips spread!

You see, the size of your body is connected in part to how much you weigh. And both size and weight are affected by lifestyle factors such as … What you eat. How much you eat. Food preparation. Family influences. Cultural practices. Exercise habits.

Therefore, if your diet consists of high calorie, fat-laden, sugar-infested food. And you consider exercise to be the act of flipping the remote while flopped on the couch … or getting up and going to the kitchen during the commercials, you are naturally going to be heavier than if you lead a healthier lifestyle that encompasses good eating and exercise habits.

But (and this is a very big *but*!) …

You have to realize that good eating and exercise habits *will not* change the basic shape of your thighs, stomach or _____. However, they will enable you to have the best-looking stomach/ thighs/ _____ your body can naturally own! And therein lies the key to your personal health, beauty and happiness.

Accepting your god-given body for what it is and doing the best you can with what you've got!

NOT FOR SALE AT ANY PRICE

Now are you thinking, "What's so earth-shattering about that? It only makes sense, doesn't it?"

Yes, it makes perfect sense! But not, unfortunately, to chronic weight watchers and worriers. This is one equation where the variables will not factor out in their favour. Because the sum of their bodily figures will never add up to a perfect "10," no matter how hard they diet and exercise to try and change their configuration. Consequently, they have tremendous difficulty accepting themselves and their "imperfect" body parts.

That was my problem.

For the longest time (twenty years, in fact), I refused to accept that the slim hips I wanted at all costs were simply *not* available to me *at any price!*

Hence, I was unable to "see" and appreciate those parts of my body that were beautiful (body parts I *did not* "earn," but were granted to me at birth!) ... my flat stomach (courtesy of my dad); my shapely calves and ankles (from my mom); my slim arms, my lovely skin; my smile.

Nor could I fully appreciate all of the miraculous aspects of my body and life that had nothing to do with outer beauty, but were of vital importance. The fact that I could see, and run, and hear, and speak. That I was blessed with good health. That I was deeply loved. Instead, my thoughts swirled perversely around my fat hips and how I could rid myself of them!

FOOD FOR THOUGHT

Why are we so dissatisfied with, and critical of, our bodies?

I mean, why can't we focus on our good bodily features rather than dwell upon those we don't and can't have?!

 FINAL FOOD FOR THOUGHT ON BODY STAMP

Unfortunately, those of us who are not naturally endowed with the long, lithe look considered beautiful today, find ourselves fighting a losing battle. We are dieting as fast as we can, and exercising as fast as we can without the results we so desperately covet. Despite our most diligent efforts, being the proud owner of a "perfect" figure continues to elude and delude us.

Why?!

Because we are fighting genetics! ... By striving to attain a body we were just not born with — a smooth, sleek, ultraslim body (with large firm breasts) that is physically impossible for the majority of us to own.

And it is such a waste of time and energy! It's like trying to change the shape of the moon, the length of our legs, the width of our heads.

SELF-ACCEPTANCE

Ultimately, we have to realize that we were not all created from the same body mold. Each of us is a unique individual with our own specific body stamp.

And once we acknowledge this, we can move forward to accept those physical attributes we *can not* change (inherited body build and weight distribution, for example); and work with and around those we *can* (including body size in relation to lifestyle choices).

It is this self-acceptance, coupled with the self-determination to make the very best of what we are born with, that forms the cornerstone of a healthy relationship with food!

But, the path leading towards acceptance is blocked by an intimidating obstacle of gargantuan proportions ... our thin-obsessed, media-inculcated society that idolizes slenderness. A society where a person's beauty *and attached worth*! are measured specifically in terms of pounds and inches.

But do not fear! This next chapter will address those issues and explore how you can overcome them!

Chapter 4

Society

TODAY, "THE LOOK" IS UNMISTAKABLY LEAN, LITHE, AND BIG-BREASTED!

Throughout the ages and in different cultures, the concept of "beauty" has ranged from one end of the spectrum to the other. Take Rubens's day, for example, when the coveted "look" was round and voluptuous. We were simply born at the wrong time!

During that glorious period, *we* would have been "the chosen" ones. During that enlightened time, our fuller figures would have epitomized the em"body"ment of beauty. How ugly those Twiggy types must have felt then! Strive as they might, stuff themselves as they may, they were destined to be skinny and scrawny in a world that valued beauty in the form of curves and rolls! Today, however, we are conditioned to believe we can *never* be too thin. Today, the coveted look is unmistakably lean, lithe, and big-breasted.

In light of this, have you ever stopped to consider who the current role models of beauty really are? I mean, just exactly who is it we are dieting and exercising so earnestly to emulate?

Ironically, the "women" we see gracing fashion magazines, television screens and runways are often teenagers who possess the distinctive look of a well-endowed but otherwise skinny adolescent. Unfortunately, that "look" is the one so many females of all ages are irrationally seeking to attain. Those of us who are unique individuals with our own definitive body stamps and metabolisms.

But, is it any wonder we harbour unrealistic aspirations?

For not only are we bombarded day in and day out with images of who we should be, what we should own, and how we should look; but we are also on the receiving end of some very potent and mixed messages that permeate our lives and fuel our bodily frustration.

For example ...

THERE IT SITS, KISSED WITH PROVOCATIVE LIPS OF CHOCOLATE!

Standing in the check-out line at the supermarket, my eyes are drawn to a ladies' magazine with the same old repetitious headline screaming from the front cover, "Lose 10 pounds *easily* in just one week!"

What a joke! I mean, do you really know anyone who has lost ten pounds in one week and lived happily and thinly ever after? ... But how many of us, egged on by the dangling carrot of potential thinness, have been led to believe implausible weight loss claims?

I know I have.

There once was a time when I could not have purchased that magazine fast enough, trembling with feverish anticipation at the promise of shedding ten glorious pounds in seven short days! Today, however, after being disillusioned, demoralized and disappointed one too many times, I finally know better. Today, I am a whole lot wiser (and thinner!).

Thus, as I flip through that magazine, armed with my hard-earned wisdom and a healthy dose of scepticism, other weighted ironies jump out at me. For instance, the page opposite the proclaimed "wonder diet" boasts a life size, full colour close-up of the winning cake in the "Search for the Chocolatiest Chocolate Cake in America" Contest! There it sits, poised right before my salivating eyes, aswirl in its frosted magnificence, caressed by whipped cream and kissed with provocative lips of chocolate curls.

And therein lies the crux of our emotional tug-of-war with food!

 FOOD FOR THOUGHT

One-half of our dieting plate is laden with persistent temptation (ever present in our food-embedded world!) ... while the other is burdened with our persistent desire (sown by society and cultivated through the media) to be thin and beautiful at all costs.

Consequently, part of us wants to begin that diet that very minute to enable us to be thin enough to enjoy that forbidden food. While simultaneously, another part of us is pulled in the opposite direction by seductive thoughts of dieting sabotage tugging at our tastebuds. "Oh! How sinfully sweet a dalliance with that decadent dessert would be!"

The trouble is ... literally, we want to have our cake *and* figuratively, we want to eat it, too! *And we can't!*

WHAT ARE THE REST OF US GOING TO HAVE TO DO IN OUR ATTEMPTS TO LOOK LIKE THEM?

As I continue to peruse this magazine, I am struck by yet another irony that aptly underscores the "you can't have your cake and eat it, too" philosophy. In this case, several famous and beautiful actresses were asked how they managed to keep their much flaunted, much exposed, and much envied physiques. Their remarks are just about as revealing as their figures!

One star constantly monitors each and every morsel she puts into her mouth — even denying herself pickles (which she loves) because the salt might cause her to retain water, and a pound or two! Another actress exercises two hours daily (including weekends and holidays!) to keep her working weight down. And yet another slim beauty faithfully follows a weekly fasting regime.

Now I realize that many actresses are naturally endowed with their knockout figures. Furthermore, I understand that they have to be concerned with how they look because their livelihood depends upon it. However, what I find difficult to comprehend is that some of these women are fighting their bodies every step of the way to ensure that they are thin enough for the camera. I am surprised to discover that they, too, fall under the power of *the Almighty Scale* and are cautiously peering down each morning to see where the weight of that thin black needle will lie.

 FOOD FOR THOUGHT

If Hollywood beauties have to worry about eating a pickle or exercising obsessively in order to maintain their precious shapes; what are the rest of us going to have to do in our attempts to look like them?

Starve and exercise ourselves to death?!

And then there is this to consider.

In some instances, the bodies of the women we seek to pattern ourselves after have been artificially sculpted to perfection by the hands of a plastic surgeon or two (or three, or four!).

And if that's the case, if we are desperately dieting and exercising to duplicate women such as these who have acquired their look through surgical means, we have to ask ourselves this.

"How far are we prepared to go in our quest to achieve bodily 'perfection?' … As far as the slice of a surgeon's knife?"

MAN TO MAN

My husband has been an avid soccer player all of his life. And would you believe that *not once* in the clubhouse after a game has he witnessed one man turn to another and plaintively whine, "Do you think I'm fat?!" ... Nor has he heard a man repeatedly berate his body, or dwell endlessly upon diets and dieting. Jon says that occasionally a player will offhandedly comment, "Gotta get rid of this gut." as he reaches for another beer!

Contrast that scene to a group of female tennis players lunching after a match; or a gathering of ladies at a clothing or jewelry party. What inevitably does the topic of conversation turn to? Weight, dieting, and bodily unhappiness — naturally!

 FOOD FOR THOUGHT

Why are women more openly preoccupied with weight than men?

I mean, why is the size and shape of our bodies such an all-consuming issue for us?

I know why.

Our obsession with weight stems from the fact that we are conditioned from birth to believe we should live up to (or diet down to!) the contemporary standard of societal beauty — ultra-slimness. And in the process, we are made to feel that our personal worth is attached to our weight. Thus, if we are not long-legged and thin with nice-sized breasts, we feel something is wrong with us and, as a result, struggle blindly and relentlessly towards fitting this prepackaged mold.

FURTHER FOOD FOR THOUGHT

It is only natural that society defines, and the media portrays the current concept of beauty. However, what is so hard to understand is this. As intelligent as we are, as educated as we are (and as liberated as we like to think we are!), women swallow the "never too slim" doctrine hook, line, and sinker!

On the other hand, how many men take the bait?

How many men repeatedly aspire to attain unrealistic bodily standards and then spend an inordinate amount of time and energy worrying about it?

Very few!

But in all fairness to women, there are some fundamental physiological differences between the sexes that give men a distinct advantage in the weight department. And I think these differences (coupled with society's portrayal of physical perfection and our willingness to buy into it) play a significant role in shaping the "dietitis" mind-set that predominantly plagues females.

For example ...

Most men are able to eat more than women due to their larger size. Hence, what they eat and where it ends up on their body is not such a big issue for them, and they are less likely to be drawn into dieting.

Furthermore, women are biologically programmed to have higher percentages of body fat; body fat that exists in places we wish it didn't ... like around our hips, stomachs, thighs and derrieres! Thus, we have a heck of a time trying to get rid of this genetically assigned (but sorely unwanted) weight, and become obsessed with doing so.

And if that isn't frustrating enough, women are forced to sacrifice far more than men physically and emotionally when it comes to losing weight! ... as evidenced by this.

ALL HE DID WAS CUT BACK ON HIS BEER!

One New Year's Eve, Bev and Randy made a resolution to lose weight together. They were planning a Hawaiian vacation in late February, and both wanted to shed fifteen pounds of excess flab in the meantime. Therefore, January the first (when else?) this couple embarked upon a sensible, healthy diet and exercise program with a very tangible goal in sight — the vision of themselves hand in hand, proudly strutting along the beach in their slim, svelte bodies.

Can you predict the outcome?

Two months later, Bev (who stuck like Super glue to her diet and fitness program) had lost only ten and a half of the fifteen pounds she had hoped to shed. While Randy (who had not dieted nearly as faithfully!) dropped seventeen pounds. In fact, Randy lost most of his weight by simply cutting back on his beer intake! (Note: Randy did not stop drinking beer completely — he just didn't have as much!)

Give me a break!

 FOOD FOR THOUGHT

Why, as a rule, is it so much harder for women to lose weight than men?

Well, I think the answer lies in reproductive differences; more specifically, in the childbearing role that is biologically bestowed upon women. For if a woman becomes too thin, she doesn't ovulate and can not bear children. Furthermore, if women died easily from starvation, so would the unborn and nursing young. Thus, if a woman's body relinquished weight as readily and easily as a man's, there would be dire consequences for the procreation and preservation of the human race.

However, despite all of the inherent physiological factors that influence a female's body shape and weight, many women continue to be at odds with, and to fight against, the way their bodies naturally are. And it is this frustration, fueled by societal expectation that draws us into the web of worry and diets that ensnares our lives and our sensibilities.

(In a way, we are our own worst enemy, aren't we?)

BEER NUTS

And while we are on the topic of men, women and weight, can you tell me why it is more socially acceptable for a man to be heavier than a woman? I mean, why can a guy appear on the beach with a thirty pound spare tire bulging over his waistband — *beer in hand*! But, heaven forbid, if a woman who carries the same amount of extra weight (and has given birth to three children to boot!) walks by a group of men in her swimsuit on that very same stretch of sand. Can't you just envision "the boys" nudging one another and commenting, "How gross!" as they take another swig of beer?!

Talk about a double standard!

Here's more food for thought along those lines.

WHAT'S FOR DINNER TONIGHT, HON?

My husband Jon is a very liberated man who willingly does more housework than most men I know. But — despite that, and the fact we are both teachers who have the same university degrees and number of years' teaching experience, guess whose "job" it is to think about what we are going to eat ninety-nine per cent of the time? Moi, of course.

Lest you think this statement highly sexist and exaggerated, consider the following.

As Jon and I left the house for work one day, I asked him what he felt like having for dinner. My rationale being ... (a) I was sick and tired of making that decision (b) I could take the meat out of the freezer to defrost and (c) I wouldn't have to give supper a second thought — we could just come home and prepare it. But Jon was no help whatsoever. His simple, sleepy response was, "I can't think about dinner this early in the morning."

"Fine," I thought and left it at that. "If he can't, then why should I?"

But lo and behold when 6 o'clock rolled around and Jon started rummaging hungrily about the kitchen, he had the audacity to ask in all innocence, "Well, hon, what are we going to have for supper tonight?"

To which I could hardly suppress my sarcasm as I replied, "Oh, I don't know, sweetheart. I can't think about dinner this late in the day!"

 FOOD FOR THOUGHT

Why, in the majority of households, are women most often responsible for the food — even when they hold full-time jobs outside the home?

Is this fair?

Is it fair that wives, mothers, sisters and girlfriends have to perpetually think about food and be involved with its preparation, merely because we were born female?

I mean, I thought the days of the cave man were over; the days when men went out to hunt and women gathered berries and prepared the food!

Furthermore, don't men and women possess the very same bodily equipment necessary for cooking — a set of eyes to read a recipe, a mind to understand instructions, and a pair of hands to carry out the work?! So why does the onus of mealmaking fall so heavily upon the plates of women … women who, more often than not, are dieting and therefore trying to keep their contact with food to a bare minimum?

And if all of this isn't hard enough to take. If we aren't already heavily overburdened and overstressed in our socially preordained relationship with food, we also have to contend with this.

IF ONLY I COULD WIRE MY JAWS SHUT AND SLEEP FOR A MONTH!

Today, wherever we turn, "food, glorious food!" confronts us. Whether walking down the aisle of a twenty-four hour superstore *lined* with every food imaginable. Or driving down a boulevard *lined* with an explosion of fast food outlets. Or watching television where the food advertisements are *lined* up to send us scurrying in the direction of the kitchen. Regardless of the time or place, food is always *lined* up to serve us at our beck and fork!

In addition, every single social function embraces food. You name it and we celebrate it! ... New Year's Eve, the Super Bowl, Valentine's Day, Easter, Mother's Day, Father's Day, a Twenty-fifth Wedding Anniversary, your boss's Retirement, a friend's Fortieth Birthday, a Christening, Thanksgiving, Christmas ... And along with the celebration, comes the "eat, drink, and be merry" syndrome. And as we know full well, there is always far too much to eat, drink, and be merry with!

Consequently, the neverending stream of temptation in our food-embedded world makes dieting downright intolerable and predictably self-defeating! So much so, that during my dieting days, I longed to take a total hiatus from socializing.

I used to dream about how wonderful it would be if I could temporarily drop out of society and live in a foodless vacuum. I felt if I could just abandon life's pressures and isolate myself from all that food for a while; *then* I would be able to kickstart my diet, lose all the weight I wanted, and henceforth be empowered to remain skinny and forever fortified against the formidable army of edibles that were constantly assaulting my better intentions.

Actually, Ruth said it best when she once stated in all seriousness, "If I could just wire my jaws shut and sleep for a month, I know I'd lose weight!"

(Isn't that the truth!... The problem, however, is how to keep it off.)

RATHER THAN WORRYING ABOUT AFFORDING OUR MEALS, WE CONCENTRATE ON AVOIDING THEM

Not only is food readily available and plentiful in today's society, but it is also very affordable. Our affluence enables most of us to purchase virtually any food we want, at any time, and in any amount. It also affords us the luxury of thinking about food in terms of our figures rather than our survival. Therefore, instead of wondering where our next meal is going to come from, we concentrate on avoiding it. Rather than worrying about intaking enough calories for our daily sustenance, we concoct innovative and painless ways to minimize our consumption of them!

But, easy access to food is not all that besets dieters. Here is yet another facet of our society that adds to our bodily woes.

WITH THE PUSH OF A BUTTON

Unlike the past when people toiled from dawn to dusk merely to put food on the table, we live in a highly technological world where time-and-labour-saving devices reduce the amount of manual work we do and the number of calories we expend. Therefore, we don't have to grow the grain and knead the dough for our bread; or plant and harvest our vegetables. We don't have to raise a cow for milk and slaughter one for meat.

Instead, when we feel the urge to eat, we can hop into our car and zip down to a local fast food outlet. Or, take a frozen dinner out of the freezer, buzz it in the microwave, enjoy, and then plop the dirty plate into the dishwasher. And therein lies another paradox. All of this modern convenience gives us more spare time; but our rat race lifestyle often depletes us of the energy to do something productive with it!

Nowadays it is simply too easy and tempting to "do the couch potato." Too relaxing and destressing after working all day and fighting rush hour traffic to lay sprawled in front of the TV, remote in one hand, Doritos in the other ... barely lifting a finger to flip the channel or put chip to lip! All the while, vowing to gather up the energy and resolve to start eating and exercising "right" tomorrow. Ah yes, tomorrow!

QUICK FIX SOCIETY

And to top everything off (as if we didn't have enough to stomach on our dieting plates!), we find ourselves living in a quick fix, microwave society where we are used to having what we want — fast! Our affluence, coupled with our state of the art technology, enables us to experience immediate gratification as a regular, expected part of our lives. Thus, if we dislike wearing glasses, we avail ourselves of contact lenses. If our hair is drab and straight, we colour and perm it. If our facial skin is wrinkled, we pay a visit to the plastic surgeon.

But this quick fix, microwave mentality has a huge downside for dieters!

Because dieting is not a quick fix endeavour. On the contrary, it takes *time* to lose weight, and it takes *time* to keep it off for good!

Furthermore, dieting can not guarantee success — instant or otherwise. Consequently, it is difficult for us to accept that we may never be as thin as we wish — no matter *how much* we diet, *how much* we exercise, or *how much* money we are willing to spend! (Consider Christina Onassis. None of her millions could procure for her the slender body she desperately desired!)

FINAL FOOD FOR THOUGHT ON SOCIETY

As far as society is concerned, dieters are caught in the double bind of a classic Catch-22. On the one hand, we live in a food-embedded, technological age where less manual work is carried out and fewer calories burned. While on the other, we are faced with the personal desire fanned by societal and media motivation, to be slim in a quick fix world where we are used to getting what we want — almost instantly.

So what is a beleaguered dieter to do? ... Say, "To hell with it! What's the use? I may as well go ahead and attack that carton of Häagen-Dazs ice cream and devour the rest of those Peanut Butter Fudge Bars!"

No.

I would never advocate that. Because letting go completely prevents you from being the best you can be!

But what's the alternative? Diet and exercise even harder to try and attain that slim, svelte body beautiful?

No again.

Because the real heart of the matter is this. Regardless of a person's size and shape, our bodily dissatis"fat"tion and self-worth should not be so firmly and blindly attached to the current societal standard of beauty — that of a "perfect" adolescent Twiggy-type figure with (more often than not) a pair of overly endowed breasts!

Hold onto that image, plus the power society wields in creating, shaping and perpetuating it, as you contemplate the contents of the next chapter; a chapter that examines how to reconcile who you are with who you want to be.

Chapter 5

Body Image

ISN'T IT AMAZING HOW YOU CAN FEEL SKINNY ONE MINUTE AND FAT THE NEXT?!

Imagine yourself at an aerobic's class during a successful diet and exercise stint. There you are … feeling svelte, sexy and in control as you enthusiastically put your body through its paces. You've had no breakfast, a naked salad for lunch, and nothing since. You feel as thin as a celery stick and as light as a feather — virtually fatless. You are on top of the world!

And several hours after this *"feeling"* of being-in-control-of-my-weight euphoria, have you ever gone ahead and broken your diet by eating a certifiable No-No food, such as a Ding Dong?

"After all," your conscience reasons, "you deserve it. You've been working *so* hard at losing weight. And you have been *so* 'good!' Besides, how much harm can one little Ding Dong do anyhow?"

Well, six Ding Dongs and five pounds of guilt later, you are left mired in the sinking feeling that every single microscopic milligram of those stupid Ding Dongs has oozed its way directly to your problem area. So that immediately your stomach feels ten times larger and your hips twice as wide. Suddenly, the body that felt so slim and panther-swift moments before, now feels repulsively like a cross between a hippo and a two ton elephant!

50

FOOD FOR THOUGHT

It's unbelievable, isn't it, how we can feel thin one minute, and fat the next?!

I mean, physiologically it is impossible for us to be as fat as we feel after eating six Ding Dongs, or a dozen Oreos, or whatever our downfall might be. When analyzing the situation rationally, we know full well that our fat cells are physically incapable of burgeoning to capacity within seconds of consuming something fattening!

And yet ...

Isn't it amazing, how with each guilt-packed mouthful, our bum/ thighs/ stomach/ _____ (you fill in the spot) seems to grow larger and larger ... until we truly "feel" big and fat and ugly once again!

And therein lies the crux of the matter! How being fat, *feeling* fat, and seeing ourselves as fatter than we really are, is often exaggerated in our minds. A self-induced product of our thin obsessed "image"-inations that forms the basis of a negative *body image*.

But, what exactly is *body image*?

Body image is the mental snapshot we carry of our physical being. It is how we perceive the way we look and how those perceptions influence our feelings, attitudes and actions (most notably, our eating behaviour!).

FOOD FOR THOUGHT

How do you see yourself bodywise?

Do you feel that the tops of your legs are heavy, or that your hips are too wide, or that your stomach isn't flat enough?

51

If so, did you know that over 90% of women emotionally inflate the size and shape of their bodies?

In light of this, have you ever stopped to consider just how accurate your body image is ... and how your bodily perceptions affect your relationship with food?

Hold onto those thoughts as you meet Vicky, a classic example of someone who harbours an unrealistic body image that heavily impacts upon her eating and exercise habits.

SHE IS BEAUTIFUL, SLENDER AND MULTITALENTED — BUT!

Vicky is a person who has everything (and I mean *everything*!) going for her ... beauty, charm, intelligence, and a dynamite figure. However, despite all of this, Vicky is overly consumed with how much she weighs and how "fat" she is. Her bodily dissatis"fat"tion was pitifully highlighted one evening during a buffet dinner party.

As Vicky was settling down to eat, Roberta glanced at Vicky's plate and remarked upon the bird-size portions. In response, Vicky protested she truly wasn't hungry and proceeded to describe how earlier in the day she had pumped her exercise bike for forty-five minutes. Then remembering the party that night, she decided she'd better give herself some more caloric leverage. So, she plopped in a Jane Fonda Workout Challenge tape and went "for the burn" — not once, but *twice* — for a total of three hours! *Can you imagine*!!?

Eyeing her lithe body, Roberta and I were flabbergasted! We both thought Vicky had a terrific figure, an enviable figure. We said, "If you were any thinner, you'd look like you had just been released from a concentration camp!"

But without missing a beat, Vicky quickly retorted, "Are you kidding?! My sister-in-law and I are *exactly* the same height, and she weighs ten pounds *less* than I do!"

Something very troubling was happening here! Something that defies rationale. For Vicky is as physically perfect as any woman could possibly hope to be, but in her mind's eye (and using her sister-in-law's weight as her scale) Vicky "sees" herself as fat.

And unfortunately, this distorted body image repeatedly sows the seeds of discontent within the fertile soil of her thin conscious mind. And those seeds of unhappiness multiply, until Vicky feels compelled to "do something" about her "fat" and "ugly" body. Thus, she turns to dieting.

But that only leads to more unhappiness.

Because nine out of ten dieters fail. And Vicky is no exception … for no matter how hard she tries, she never manages to remain as thin as she ideally wishes. And this further intensifies and fuels her bodily frustration until she is driven to diet again. Which predictably ends in failure and generates a whole new wave of negative emotions to compound those that already exist.

Talk about a self-defeating, self-destructive cycle! All of which is *self-imposed*!

 FOOD FOR THOUGHT

Why is Vicky's body image so badly out of focus? I mean, why does she emotionally magnify her bodily "imperfections" and "fatness?"

(Sound familiar?)

Furthermore, why does she set such extraordinary standards for herself?

The answers are rooted in society.

For ever since we were young, we have been conditioned to believe that to be thin is to be beautiful — in fact, the thinner the better. And the message is so strong and so relentless that we begin to associate our personal worth with our weight. As a result, we place ourselves under constant pressure to diet and exercise our bodies into something they can never be — long-legged, thin, and big-breasted!

Up until recently, I was so wrapped up in dieting and exercising as fast as I could to try and achieve that perfect body, I didn't stop to ask myself if it really was physically possible for me to attain.

 FOOD FOR THOUGHT

Just how realistic are your bodily expectations?

Moreover, what size and shape would you ideally like to be?

In view of that, have you *ever* had a perfect figure? If so, when ... five, ten, fifteen years ago? And for how long ... one day (June 13, 1982), three months, a year?

Furthermore, when you were those ten, twenty, thirty _____ pounds lighter, were you perfectly happy with your body at the time? Or would you liked to have been just a little bit thinner?

Chances are, you didn't think you were quite thin enough (or perfect enough) even then, right? And yet ... what you wouldn't give to be that weight today!

 FURTHER FOOD FOR THOUGHT

Considering all of the weight watching and worrying you have done during your life, do you honestly think you are physically equipped with a body that is capable of fitting the current societal mold of bodily perfection?

And if so, just how on earth are you going to make your size and shape conform to that standard when all of your previous efforts have failed to produce a permanently thin body, let alone a "perfect" one?

I have a better idea.

Why not let go of your quest for the perfect figure and start right here and now to begin seeing your body in a kinder, gentler, more realistic way?

Here's the first step in that direction. The first step towards developing a more accurate body image tempered by realistic bodily expectations. It involves looking objectively beyond our own bodies into the real world, a world of "imperfection."

THERE WAS NARY A PERFECT BODY AMONGST US

The next time you are at the beach, the pool, or in a changing room, take a moment to mentally step back and observe the people around you. And in doing so, I want you to count the number of *women* you see who actually have a "perfect" figure! And by perfect, I do not mean someone who is slim and looks great in jeans. I mean a true blue voluptuous bathing beauty ... a Bo Derek in a thong bikini. Someone whose body is so sleek and toned, it could be examined stark naked under the glare of flood-lights and the scrutiny of a magnifying glass without revealing a trace of cellulite or ounce of fat!

Does even *one* person qualify?!

 FOOD FOR THOUGHT

Realistically, just how many females other than movie stars, models, and twelve year olds truly have perfectly shaped, perfectly lean, cellulite-free bodies?

So why in heaven's name are 99.9% of us attempting to emulate that .1%?

(Aren't we being just a tad unrealistic?!)

IN "FAT" UATION

In reality, very few people are naturally endowed with a "perfect" figure. And even fewer of us are capable of having one — regardless of how faithfully we count our calories and pump our Reeboks. Furthermore, society's standard of bodily perfection has been elevated to such an unattainable height, that even those who have a perfect figure don't think it is perfect enough! Here's a perfect example of that.

SHE LOOKS FAT IN A BATHING SUIT?!

Of all the beautiful women in the public eye today, I think Christie Brinkley is one of *the* most gorgeous. Her fresh natural beauty and radiance, coupled with her fabulous figure, have made her the envy of millions of women (not to mention the object of desire for countless men!). Who could possibly ask for more in the good looks department? ... Well, I was absolutely flabbergasted one evening while watching Christie during a television interview. As the conversation turned to her swimsuit work, Christie admitted to being self-conscious of her "big" hips. So self-conscious, in fact, that she deliberately tried to disguise them when she posed.

Now it was one of "those" poses (where Christie was trying to hide her big hips) that ended up staring so provocatively from the front cover of *SPORTS ILLUSTRATED!*

Give me a break!

FOOD FOR THOUGHT

How could someone who has such a quintessential figure. Someone world famous for her knockout face and body, possibly be unhappy with her hips?

Furthermore ...

How could Christie carry such an inaccurate image of those hips in her head? ... When her body epitomizes what the rest of us are all dieting and exercising so diligently to duplicate!

THE HEART OF THE MATTER

Sadly, it seems that no matter what our size and shape (or how perfect!), few of us are completely satisfied with our bodies, are we?

As a result, how can we ever feel truly good about ourselves when we are so unhappy with, and overly critical of, how we look?

The answer is simple. We can't ... until we stop defining ourselves (and those around us) in physical terms. Until we stop judging ourselves and assessing our self worth in terms of how much we weigh and how big or little our hips/ stomachs/ thighs/ _____ measure. Because when all of our emotions are wrapped up in the size and shape of our bodies, we lose sight of who we really are and what is really important. We lose sight of the "whole" person and reduce ourselves (and others) to the superficial sum of our body parts.

However, changing our mind-set to get past the purely physical requires courage, conviction and a true desire to think and feel differently. In essence, it involves a willingness to relinquish an old value system and replace it with another ... which is no small feat!

*But it can be done. **And you can do it**!*

In order to succeed, you must undergo some heavy soul-searching. Honest, often painful soul-searching that takes you beneath the surface of skin deep beauty to come face to face with the real heart of the matter — accepting yourself for who you are and treating yourself with the respect, kindness and dignity you deserve!

And therein lies the crux of the issue. ***The change must come from the inside out, not the outside in!***

Because developing a better body image does not involve dieting to alter your outer self and *then* feeling good within. Oh no, developing a better body image works in the reverse. It begins by feeling good about who you are right here and now (focusing upon your assets, not your shortcomings); accepting your body for what it is ("imperfections" and all); and acknowledging that which you do not have the power to change.

And in the process, you must be prepared to shed the belief that, "If I was thin, everything in my life would be perfect."

Because that is only wishful thinking.

How so?

Consider this.

 FOOD FOR THOUGHT

Will being thin make you a better/kinder/more intelligent person? Will it miraculously make your financial/marital/work related problems disappear?

Moreover ...

If you were given Christie Brinkley's body right here and now, wouldn't you still be the same person inside with the same strengths and weaknesses, the same attributes and flaws, and ... the same eating habits?

FURTHER FOOD FOR THOUGHT

What really needs to change is not the size or shape of your body, but your capacity for self-acceptance.

For if you are whole and well on the inside, how you look on the outside won't carry such an inordinate amount of weight. And this balance between your inner and outer self leads to a healthier and happier relationship with food.

Here's what happens when you don't make that connection.

BUT MRS. DINGLE, MEN LIKE WOMEN WITH BIG HIPS!

Several years ago, while still whirling in circles on the trying-to-change-my-body-shape merry-go-round, I decided to seek professional help. I knew I had a problem with weight and dieting and I wanted to get to the bottom of it *once and for all*!

With this conviction, I approached my family doctor and explained my situation. But he was surprised and reluctant to refer me to a psychiatrist. After listening to what I had to say, he sighed knowingly, shook his head, and said patiently but patronizingly, "Pauline, a calorie is a calorie. Your body does *not* manufacture them. What you put into your mouth is responsible for your weight."

Then he put his hand on my shoulder, looked me straight in the eye and said, "If you want to be thinner, you'll just have to stick more faithfully to counting each and every calorie."

Rather than argue the validity of that comment (little did the good doctor know he was dispensing calorie counting advice to a virtual walking caloric computer!), I managed to convince him that the root of my problem lay deeper than that. He acquiesced and recommended a therapist to me. I was excited, happy, and hopeful to think I could finally sit down with a professional, examine my obsession with food and thinness, and conquer it — **forever!**

In my zealous anticipation, I had actually compiled a list of possible reasons for my behaviour. Was I "stuck" in the oral stage? Was I too much of a perfectionist? Was everything in my life so good I needed something to worry about? Did I have a subconscious sexual problem?

I was eager, expectant and willing to be "cured!"

Unfortunately, however, upon seeing the psychiatrist for the first time, I was not overly impressed. In a dingy room with the curtains drawn on a glorious autumn day, an older man (barely visible through the clouds of smoke created by his incessant cigarette puffing!) sat before me. I couldn't help but think, "I wonder if he's worried about being 'stuck' in the oral stage?"

Furthermore, he looked at me as if I had rocks in my head when I produced my list of probable causes. (This should have been my second clue as to the value of his therapy … his chain-smoking being the first!)

However, anxious to address my problem, I tucked these initial reservations aside and openly discussed my life with him (family, husband, work, breast size, etc.). And thus, after several visits, the psychiatrist concluded that I was a very happy, well-adjusted individual; but then he said something I will never forget.

In a matter-of-fact monotone, he stated, "Mrs. Dingle, I do not understand why you are so unhappy with your body. After all, *men like women with big hips*."

I could not believe my ears! … I looked at him dumbfounded!?! It was all I could do to restrain myself from leaping across the desk, putting my hands around his throat, and screaming at the top of my lungs, "*What*?! I don't care what men think. I don't want to have these big hips! *I hate my fat hips*!! … That's why I'm here, you imbecile!"

Needless to say, that session was my last! And what did I immediately proceed to do? For those caught in the self-defeating cycle of non-acceptance, there are only two options — to pig out again, or diet again. And this time, I chose the later. I chose to go back to the dieting drawing board to try and lose those big hips ... *big hips men liked so much*, but that I hated with all of my heart and soul!

I AM WHAT I AM

In retrospect, I wish I had never started dieting. I wish instead that I had learned to accept my body fifteen pounds and twenty years ago. I wish that I had demagnified my imperfections, focused upon my assets, and not wasted so much of my precious time and energy struggling to achieve a body I did not have at thirteen, let alone thirty. But, blinded self-consciously by the size of my hips in comparison to the width society deemed desirable, I steadfastly refused to look beyond them.

 FOOD FOR THOUGHT

Do you have negative tunnel vision as far as your body is concerned? I mean, do you tend to see only what is physically "wrong" with you?

If so, compose a list of bodily features you like about yourself ... your nose, hair, cheek bones, waistline.

Then, go to a full length mirror. And from now on (and as difficult as it may be at first)!, I want you to zoom in on those "good" body parts. And in the process, don't allow your eyes be drawn to the hips/ stomach/ thighs/ _____ you hate so much. Because dwelling repeatedly and exclusively upon your "imperfections" will only serve to heighten your feelings of dissatis"fat"tion (feelings that keep us firmly seated on the merry-go-round of dieting!).

Now after identifying your physical assets, take stock of the special intrinsic qualities you possess ... such as kindness, intelligence, humour, loyalty.

And then, from this point forward in your life, try seeing yourself more in those terms. Because once you succeed in highlighting your inner beauty along with your physical attributes, they will gradually overshadow the "less than perfect" aspects of your size and shape. My girlfriend Cathy is a good example of this. She has a large body, *but*! ... such a dynamite personality, and so many other truly beautiful features (her hair, eyes, laugh) and she dresses so distinctively, that I honestly don't see her as being anything but beautiful!

In essence, Cathy's philosophy is, "I am what I am — a full figured woman. And regardless of my size, I deserve to treat myself nicely and be treated nicely because ... I am worth it! And besides, there is a lot more to me and to life than how much I weigh."

And because Cathy feels so good about herself, it shines through and others can't help but see her in a positive light!

However, viewing yourself (and those around you) in less physical terms will initially feel very strange and somewhat overwhelming. For you will be striving to overcome many powerful forces, including the most powerful of all — the obsessive desire (fueled by society and perpetuated by the media) to be model thin.

But, *you can do it!*

Because ultimately you are the one in control. You alone have the power to feel positively towards yourself and others. And although your ability to act and feel this way may be difficult and deliberate at first; eventually, these actions and feelings will become more natural, and a natural part of you. And subsequently, you will be released from the overriding need to diet and exercise your body into something it can never be — a societal "10."

IS IT ANY WONDER?

But once we accept ourselves for who we are bodywise and let go of the negative body images and feelings that catapult us into dieting, how do we resist falling prey to the unrealistic standard of bodily perfection that makes us feel inadequate and compels us to diet once again?

I mean, how do we keep our body in proper perspective and proportion, when we are emotionally saturated by a society that places too much value — *a disproportionate, unhealthy amount of value*! — upon a thin body?

Again, this will not be easy.

I should know.

For even after coming to terms with my body (and writing a book about the process!), I still have to guard against the pervasive desire to acquire the "perfect" figure. And *when the urge strikes* (which it does!), I emotionally grab a hold of myself ... by bringing my bodily expectations down to earth and focusing upon my assets, not my shortcomings!

And you must do the same!

You must detach yourself from the societally motivated, self-propelled current of bodily unhappiness and dissatisfaction that churns within you and gives rise to the unrealistic expectation of bodily perfection. Because this unhealthy stream of consciousness will only suck you into the whirlpool of dieting. (And we all know where that leaves us, don't we?)

Now, let's turn to something that will induce positive feelings and encourage controlled eating behaviour. Something that has nothing at all to do with dieting or exercising, but can make you feel good about yourself almost immediately!

PAULINE, EVERYONE LOOKS FAT IN THOSE TYPE OF PANTS — EVEN BONA FIDE BONERACKS!

Isn't it amazing how certain clothes can make us *feel* fat or thin?!

Take my two white cotton summer pants, for example. One pair is tighter fitting with slimming lines shaped by darts and small hidden side pockets. The other pair can best be described as harem pants, with yards of material cascading from a dropped pleated waist to a gathered cuff at the ankles.

I had purchased these harem pants during a fat period when I was experiencing tremendous difficulty finding any pants to fit. While they are extremely comfortable (like pyjama bottoms), I always feel like an absolute cow in them! Even now, when I am fifteen to twenty pounds lighter, the moment I put them on, I "feel" fat — *instantly*!?

And that's what is so incredible! I can slip into my slim-line slacks and feel perfectly thin one minute; and then replace them with my harem pants and feel indescribably fat and ugly the next!

And do you know what happens when I *"feel"* fat?

When I *feel* fat, I eat "fatly."

And therein lies the significance … the power of clothes in terms of the immediate impact they have upon our bodily perceptions, and how we feel and eat as a result!

 FOOD FOR THOUGHT

I mean, isn't it true that when you are on a successful dieting roll, feeling in control and enthused about your slimmer self, that it much easier to stay on the dieting straight and narrow?

Because when we perceive we look good, it makes us feel good; which in turn enables us to "behave" when it comes to food, doesn't it?

On the other hand ...

When we feel big and fat and ugly (after pigging out, or trying on clothes — swimsuits are a killer!, not to mention baggy harem pants!) ... isn't it strange how this feeling of fatness can make us want to eat even more?

Perhaps when we "feel" fat (whether real, exaggerated, or imagined), we overeat to psychologically justify having that tummy or those saddle bag hips, or our excess weight wherever it may be. Perhaps, when we are not in the process of trying to diet our fat away, the act of overeating verifies that, "Yes, I deserve to be overweight, because I am a big fat wimp who doesn't have an ounce of self-control! And as such, the punishment for my 'crime' is a justifiable lifetime sentence to solitary confinement with my huge hips/ tummy/ _____!"

Hence, in an attempt to escape that dreadful decree, we embark upon another guilt-wracking diet!

But one of the ways to combat the negative feelings of fatness that shame us into dieting, is to wear clothes that make us feel attractive *right at this very moment in time*!

Now I realize this is far easier said than done. I know how downright difficult and exasperating it can be to find clothes that fit, let alone ones that make you look great! (After all, I once tried on twenty-seven pair of pants in four major department stores one afternoon before I finally found a pair that fit!) But, regardless of how humiliating and discouraging and time-consuming the prospect, you must force yourself to go out and shop for clothes that flatter your figure right now! Believe me, your efforts will be rewarded a thousand fold!

Because the *style* and *colour* and *patterning* of clothing; combined with strategically placed, distinctive accessories (like eye-catching earrings!) can make a world of difference in shaping your body as well as your feelings. Moreover, when you feel good in what you are wearing, there is a natural tendency to spruce up other facets of your appearance, such as your hair and makeup. And all of these factors play a significant role in raising your self-esteem and increasing your capacity to deal more normally with food!

And as a result, you will not be anxiously awaiting the unpromised tomorrows when you wistfully hope to fit into that two piece bathing suit or those size 9 designer jeans hanging expectantly at the back of your closet in anticipation of your future thinness. Perhaps one day you will be able to wear them. Perhaps you will not. Either way, your current happiness will not be pinned so tenuously upon items of clothing that are useless to you at this point in time.

PAINTED ON JEANS

Now, here's one last note about dressing for your eating success.

Avoid wearing clothes for the hips you wished you had, or the size you used to be (whether larger or smaller). For if you have lost weight and your pants are so baggy you are swimming in them; or if you have gained and your jeans are so tight they look painted on, there is something wrong with the way you perceive yourself. And if that's the case, you need to reread this chapter and rethink your bodily perceptions until you can get your head around a more accurate body image. Because a realistic body image constitutes another fundamental building block in the foundation of a normal relationship with food.

FINAL FOOD FOR THOUGHT ON BODY IMAGE

While it is healthy for us to care about our appearance (and while we would all like to be as beautiful as possible!), it is unhealthy to focus so exclusively upon the physical that we become one dimensional and lose sight of the whole person. Furthermore, it is equally unhealthy to harbour a distorted body image that is umbilically tied to the unrealistic expectations that suck us into the quicksand of dieting.

However, if we do find ourselves caught in this self-defeating cycle of dissatis"fat"tion and unhappiness, there is a way to break free and move beyond it. In order to liberate ourselves from the emotional chains that bind our thinking and sensibilities; we need to look past the purely physical to see ourselves and others in a different, more positive light. In essence, we need to shed the self-imposed, societal cocoon of superficiality that circumscribes our vision to enable the true beauty within each of us to emerge.

If we don't, we will continue to feel miserable and inadequate ... until, hopefully, these feelings become so uncomfortable that they act as a catalyst for change. A change that involves letting go of an unhealthy value system (a value system that bestows a disproportionate amount of respect and adulation upon a thin body); and replacing it with one that lets the inner beauty of a person's heart and soul shine through!

Chapter 6

Diets and Dieting

HOW LONG HAS SHE BEEN DIETING?

When Ethel and her husband came for dinner last summer, we went to great lengths to prepare a special calorie-light, fat-free meal. You see, Ethel was involved in a diet program where her food intake was strictly dictated and daily monitored. Her resolve to lose the extra weight was strengthened and encouraged by a doctor who suggested that Ethel's troubling arthritis might improve if she was thinner. Ethel, by the way, is in her seventies.

On the evening of our gathering, Ethel was feeling proud of herself and justifiably so! Having dropped twenty-six of her targeted thirty pounds, the light at the end of her dieting tunnel was looming larger and brighter! As we sat and chatted over pre-dinner drinks (water with a twist of lemon for Ethel), the conversation inevitably turned towards her weight watching success. It was then, that Ethel's husband Bob piped up with an ironically humorous and illuminating anecdote.

With a grin on his face and a twinkle in his eye he said, "You know, after church the other day, a fellow parishioner tapped my arm and exclaimed enthusiastically, 'Wow, Ethel looks *fantastic*!! … How long has she been dieting?'" Without a moment's hesitation, I replied, "Oh, for about forty years now!"

GIVE THE WHEEL A WHIRL!

"Step right up to the 'lucky' Dieter's Wheel of Fortune. Go ahead! It's simple. All you have to do is give the wheel a whirl. And then stand back as it spins round and round past one diet after another after another. And as it circles, allow yourself to dream about the day your thinness will become a reality — forever!! Click, click ... click ... the needle is slowing down! It's stopped. Let's see where it has landed!"

WHAT A FEELING!

Evelyn lost so much weight the "right" way, the sensible way, that she was offered a job with her weight loss company!

Evelyn's road to success began when her bodily shame and frustration drove her to embark upon a year of committed dieting! Determined to make this the "diet to end all of her diets," she dutifully weighed and measured every morsel of food that entered her mouth. Time after time, day after monotonous dieting day, Evelyn resisted temptation by denying herself the likes of Deluxe Pizzas, Banana Splits, and Bacon Double Cheeseburgers with fries.

Instead, she staunchly stuck to her eating regime; chomping on rabbit food with a vengeance when the urge to overeat overcame her. And neither a drop of alcohol, nor mouthful of milk shake passed between her guarded lips. Oh no! Evelyn limited her liquids to black coffee and water.

And thus, Evelyn felt an overwhelming (and well deserved!) sense of personal satisfaction and euphoria when she finally accomplished her long awaited, hard-fought goal. At last she could shop in a department store and buy "normal" clothes. *What a feeling*! At last she could slip into a pair of blue jeans. *What an accomplishment*! Finally, she could appear on the beach in a bathing suit. *What a moment*!

But ...

What a disappointment! For today, Evelyn is obese (very obese) again!

 FOOD FOR THOUGHT

How many people do you know who have lost weight (regardless of the amount) and kept it off for the rest of their lives?!

One or two? Several, at the most?

Contrast that figure to the number of people you know who have not been able to keep their dieted weight off.

Is there really any comparison?!

Unfortunately, as most of us have experienced firsthand, nine out of ten dieters fail ... which leads us to the sixty-four thousand dollar question, **"Why?!"**

The answer is multifaceted; the reasons often interrelated. Let's begin by summarizing five major causes evident in previous chapters.

DIETING FAILURE REASON #1

Dieters gain weight because they overeat after the deprivation of dieting. It's a simple matter of cause and effect.

DIETING FAILURE REASON #2

Dieters inadvertently force their metabolisms to become more energy efficient and "famine" sensitive.

DIETING FAILURE REASON #3

Dieters do not accept their genetically predetermined body stamps. They foolishly struggle against their biological molding in an attempt to become a body they weren't born to be.

DIETING FAILURE REASON #4

Dieters can not withstand the neverending stream of temptation that exists in our food-embedded world.

DIETING FAILURE REASON #5

Dieters set unrealistic goals; they fall victim to society's unhealthy in"fat"uation with thinness.

Now, hold onto those reasons while we explore yet others …

I LOST THIRTY-FOUR (and a half!) POUNDS EATING CHEF SALADS

I was introduced to Barbara at a dinner party one evening. During the course of our conversation, she confided to me (a perfect stranger) that two years ago she lost thirty-four and a half pounds by eating Chef's Salads. "But," she said with a sigh, "you wouldn't believe it by looking at me now would you?"

She then shrugged, laughed a little nervously, and stated somewhat sheepishly, "Once I stopped eating Chef's Salads, I began to regain the weight." Then she sighed and added, "This morning I tipped the scales at my very heaviest. I guess I'll just have to start eating those darn Chef's Salads again."

Unfortunately for Barbara, she couldn't start eating Chef's Salad that night — it wasn't featured at the dinner table!

FOOD FOR THOUGHT

Can you (or do you want to!) ... eat primarily Chef's Salads for the rest of your life ?!

LOSE WEIGHT "FAST"

Michelle lost twenty-three pounds on a diet that involved fasting. It went like this. Begin by eating *nothing* for three days. Then, simply(?) fast one day a week for the rest of your life. This worked beautifully for Michelle ... for eight and a half months. Today, however, she is thirty pounds heavier and extremely upset with herself. She laments, "Every morning I look in the mirror and say, 'You've **got** to take this weight off.' But obviously, it's not important enough for me to do something about or I would. I know what I should do! I need to go back on that fasting diet again, but ... I just don't seem to have the willpower."

No willpower?! No wonder! Have you ever tried not eating for an entire day, let alone for the three required to kick-start this diet?! It's no small feat, I can assure you! And yet, Michelle berates herself because she is unable to face the prospect again?!

(Why do we continually place such intense, unrealistic pressure upon ourselves?)

FOOD FOR THOUGHT

Can you (or do you want to!) ... fast on and off for the rest of your life?!

BRING ON THE MARGARITAS!

Maureen introduced me to an Imitation Mayo Diet — the one where you eat so many eggs, tomatoes, and grapefruit over a fourteen day period that eventually the sight of them makes you sick!

I can vividly recall when the two of us were on our third day of "Mayo-ing" it together. We were watching the news while eating our dinner of (surprise!), "All the eggs, tomatoes, and grapefruit you desire! … Go ahead. Indulge!" the caption read. (*Indulge*?! *Give me a break*!! The mere thought makes my diet-battered stomach roll nervously over in its weight watching grave!)

Anyhow, on that particular evening the news was full of woe. There was a story about the armament buildup between the Soviet Union and the United States and its associated threat of nuclear war. There was a piece highlighting the Protestant and Catholic unrest in Northern Ireland. And another chilling exposé about people starving to death in a drought-stricken African country.

On and on the depressing realities unfolded. So much so, that halfway through the program, Maureen and I turned to one another in unison, and chorused, "My God! We'd better scrap this awful 'meal' and have some Margaritas and Mexican food before the whole world falls to pieces!"

Needless to say, we dropped our forks mid-bite and made a beeline for our favourite restaurant, where we proceeded to satiate our appetites (and our fears!) by pigging out Mexican-style. And what do you think we did bright and early the next morning? … In retrospect, it is so predictably absurd I can hardly type the words!

Yes, fueled by our guilt and desire to be thinner, we embarked upon the same diet — again! *Can you believe it*!?

And can you also believe that to this day, Maureen continues to put her faith into that diet by yo-yoing on and off it, even though she has yet to maintain her weight loss permanently … *and I have*!

Can you (or do you want to!) ... eat primarily toma-toes, grapefruit and eggs (as much as your little old heart desires!) for the rest of your life?!

OH, WHAT A DIET!

I was thrilled for Emily when she lost 27 1/2 pounds! But ... flabbergasted to learn at a summer barbeque that she wasn't "allowed" to have a slice of watermelon. (As this was my first exposure to a lo-carb diet, I was unaware that fruit is chock-full of those "fattening" carbohydrates!) Needless to say, Emily looked terrific after shedding the excess baggage. That is, until I saw her at a party six months later when she asked if I had a safety pin ... her pant zipper had burst from all the weight she had regained. (Yuk!)

However, I'm getting ahead of myself here. The day after that barbeque, Emily's svelte body had my dieting engines revved. Her initial success had opened my eyes to the virgin territory of an untried diet and I was trembling with the anticipa-tion of potential thinness. What the heck, I could give up water-melon *forever* if it meant I could be skinny! (Too bad it's really not that simple!)

There I sat in my sister-in-law's kitchen, freshly purchased diet book in one hand, and a tin of diet pop in the other ... exclaiming gleefully to Lucy, "Would you believe that I can have all the beef I want — even fattening Prime Rib?! As much lobster drenched in butter as I desire! Plus, scrambled eggs and bacon galore."

Oh, what a diet! Oh, what a feeling! Oh, what a waste of time!

For I lasted a total of three days and one morning on that stupid diet, which ended prematurely when I wolfed down six

74

Raisin Bran Muffins (megacarbohydrate No-No's!) in the space of ten minutes!! I ashamedly remember standing in the kitchen amidst the flurry of a feeding frenzy and a shower of crumbs, cramming one after another of those delicious, nutritious muffins into my mouth as fast as I could.

I just couldn't help myself!

 FOOD FOR THOUGHT

Can you (or do you want to!) … eat primarily high protein food for the rest of your live?!

MILK SHAKE MADNESS

Karen proudly shed eighteen ugly pounds on a diet where she had a milk shake for breakfast, a milk shake for lunch, and a "sensible" supper. Well, it took Karen just over a month to lose the weight, and two to regain it.

But this setback only strengthened her conviction, and prompted her to give the Dieting Wheel another whirl. This time Karen landed on a program where she dropped twenty pounds (and eight hundred and thirty-seven dollars!) on prepackaged food. However, three months after the fat, she was twenty-five pounds heavier. But not to fear, Karen was no quitter!

She next got her hands on The Israeli Army Diet. (No, she didn't have to fly to Israel and enlist — although by this time she was so frantic to lose weight, I wouldn't have put it past her!) On this particular diet, one food is eaten for the entire day. Day 1 was apples, I believe, any variety. Day 2 was chicken. And so on and so forth. Was Karen successful this time? I mean, don't you think that by now she deserved some measure of success?

Unfortunately, one doesn't have to be psychic to predict the outcome. For today, despite all of her exhaustive efforts, Karen continues to be unhappy and overweight.

FOOD FOR THOUGHT

Can you (or do you want to!) ... yo-yo from one diet and weight to another for the rest of your life?!

"I'M GOING FOR IT TONIGHT, DING!"

Bob, a fellow teacher, was the first man I had ever met who was seriously caught up in dietitis — big time! ... As were sitting on a beach supervising a class outing, Bob looked down at his stomach and commented in disgust, "Just look at this gut, will ya. I can't stand it anymore! I'm starting another diet Monday and I am getting rid of this 'sucker' once and for all."

I tried not to stare at his protruding "sucker" as he continued in earnest, "You know, Pauline, last year I lost forty-one pounds. But," he added ruefully as he patted his paunch, "I've slowly but surely gained it all back — again! I *never* seem to be able to keep the weight off!"

Consequently, that Monday, Bob took the diet pill route. And for several months, he successfully navigated the twists and turns of non-stop dieting. He lost a lot of weight, looked terrific, and was very proud of himself and his body. Then came Christmas and our staff party. I have a vivid recollection of Bob that evening.

It was midnight. And many of the guests had left, when I witnessed Bob standing at the buffet table literally inhaling any food he could lay his hands on. Sensing my watchful eye, he looked up with a momentary flicker of guilt. But quickly shrugging any misgivings aside, he stated emphatically, "I can't help it. I'm going for it tonight, 'Ding!'"(my nickname).

I responded as if talking to a child, "Why don't you just put some food on a plate and sit down and enjoy it? And then *do not*, under any circumstances, come near this table again!"

But my words were to no avail. As Bob proceeded to shovel food into his mouth at machine-gun pace, he managed to muffledly blurt out, "No. I'm going for it tonight, Ding!"

I sighed and walked away, fervently wishing I could do something to stop him. Needless to say, I saw Bob at school on Monday morning and he was back on his diet and back on his diet pills. Needless to say, during the following two years, I never did see Bob get rid of his "gut" for good. He would "lose" it and regain it, and lose it and gain it back again.

 FOOD FOR THOUGHT

Can you (or do you want to!) ... subject your body to diet pills for the rest of your life?!

"FREE" FOODS

Susan's problem was the late afternoon munchies which she prudently tried to placate by stuffing herself full of raw vegetables. Upon arriving at my house for dinner one evening, she proudly announced that she had just squashed the overwhelming urge to attack a pound of Maple Walnut Fudge by consuming a whole head of cauliflower instead. Now while I applauded her conviction to substitute a more nutritious and less fattening food for the calorie-laden candy, I inwardly shuddered.

Just how long could Susan continue to appease her appetite by munching upon truckloads of raw vegetables? Furthermore, what was she going to do when she found herself in a situation where those veggies were simply not readily at hand?

But that night Susan was so proud of her "accomplishment," I didn't have the heart to rain on her food parade. (Besides, I knew sooner or later, she would discover the raw truth for herself.)

Now please don't get me wrong! I am not negating the "diet"ary importance of fresh vegetables. On the contrary, I can't say enough about their phenomenal nutritional and hunger abating value! But that notwithstanding, I'd like you to chew on this for a moment.

Susan's cauliflower binge brought to mind one of my former diets where carrots and celery were designated "free" foods. Given this licence to eat, I proceeded to chomp my way through a twenty-five pound bag of carrots (Bugs Bunny-style!), only to turn a definitive shade of yellowy-orange from an overdose of beta carotene ... and to find myself in the dentist chair with a cracked tooth. My incessant need to be constantly biting on something had finally taken its physical toll!

 FOOD FOR THOUGHT

Can you (or do you want to!)... bombard your body with copious amounts of "free" foods for the rest of your life?!

IT'S ONLY FOURTEEN SHORT DAYS!

Now let's give the Dieting Wheel one last spin before we stop to reflect upon more reasons for the failure of dieters.

George, like Bob (of "I'm going for it tonight, Ding" fame), is untypical for a male because he is constantly weight watching and worrying. In reality, George is a very handsome young man of average size and build. But, unfortunately, he doesn't see himself that way. All he sees is his "fat" and "ugly" (George constantly uses those words to describe himself) body which he hides beneath baggy clothes, wishing all the while he could look like his classmate Brandon ... tall and lean in a skintight pair of jeans!

One spring, George desperately sought to shed some weight for his upcoming Senior Class Trip (a week at a beach resort). He lamented, "I want to be happy with my body. And," he stated with conviction, "I *don't* want people to see how 'fat' and 'ugly' I look in a bathing suit."

Thus, in order to be 'thin' and 'beautiful' for the event, George opted to go on one of "those" egg, grapefruit, and tomato based diets.

Now before George embarked upon his weight loss mission, I tried to torpedo it. As a former unsuccessful "Mayo-er" (remember the abysmal attempts of Maureen and myself), I thought I might be able to discourage him. But my words fell on deaf ears. George was determined to carry out his plan of attack. I guess the shimmering promise of potential victory in the battle of his bulge proved far more captivating than my old war stories of defeat. Let's see what happened ...

I first saw George on the morning of Day 3 as he was sitting down to a breakfast of poached eggs and grapefruit (as much as he could eat — lucky him!). Everything was going according to plan *except* George confided, "I'm starting to get a little sick and tired of this food." (Surprise, surprise!) However, after realizing I might misinterpret this comment as a sign of weakness, George was quick to add, "But I am definitely *not* going to quit because I *am* going to be slim amidst my classmates on the beach in three and a half week's time — *for sure!*"

I bumped into George unexpectedly during the afternoon of Day 4, when I "caught" him red-handed with a Snicker's bar. Smiling sheepishly he confessed, "My soccer team's practicing late ... and I couldn't survive without some food. I would have fainted," he justified apologetically.

When I saw George the next day, he was back on his egg, grapefruit, and tomato diet again. "But this time," he informed me, "I'm going to stick with it the entire two weeks. It's *only* fourteen days! I mean, if I am serious about wanting to lose this weight, I just have to exert more willpower."

And as he stood there reiterating various versions of, "It's *just* fourteen days. I should be able to survive that no problem." … I couldn't help but think, "Who are you trying to convince, George — me or you?"

Can you predict the outcome?

This time George lasted until midnight of Day 5 when, crazed with hunger and desire, he went on a rampage of the kitchen — attacking (among other goodies) a batch of freshly baked Peanut Butter Cookies earmarked for his little brother's class party the following morning!

And, pray tell, what do you think George proceeded to do the very next day?

Yes, he went on that same stupid diet — *again!*

Can you believe this?! (I mean, can you *really* believe it?!)

Consequently (as you might well have imagined by now!), George boarded the plane on the day of his class trip weighing exactly the same as when he began his month-long cycle of useless self-defeating yo-yo dieting.

It was all I could do to overcome the urge to say, "I told you so!"

 FOOD FOR THOUGHT

Can you (or do you want to!) … circle endlessly in the revolving-door-world of two week diets for the rest of your life?!

A SUCCESS STORY

In all fairness to the subject, there are people who go on a diet, lose weight, and live thinly ever after. Take Beth, for example. Fifteen years ago, twenty pounds heavier, and in the market for a husband, she found herself standing in a movie line-up behind two girls who were excitedly discussing the super powers of the latest wonder diet. She decided to go for it, and is happily married and still slim! to this day. However, Beth's experience is by far the exception rather than the rule.

As the multitude of unsuccessful dieting stories thus far illustrate (and believe me, they represent a mere handful of those that exist out there in the "Naked City!"), dieters have the odds heavily stacked against them. Let's drag ourselves far enough away from the Dieting Tables to objectively identify more reasons for the conspicuous absence of *Lady Luck* in The Game of Weight Loss.

DIETING FAILURE REASON #6

Dieters begin to feel ill (especially on restrictive, unbalanced diets).

Whether this is psychological or physiological in nature is debatable, but it definitely occurs. Take my first venture into the world of high protein diets, for example ... the one that ended prematurely when I went berserk with those Raisin Bran Muffins.

Initially I was thrilled to be "allowed" all of the no/low carbohydrate goodies I desired. However, after several days of exclusively eating this type of food, I began to feel positively sick and found myself passionately yearning for something else to eat (hence, my megacarbohydrate pig-out!). Unfortunately, I found out the hard way that no matter how wonderful it may sound, there is only so much steak, lobster and butter a person's mind and body can really stomach!

DIETING FAILURE REASON #7

The best made plans of dieters go astray as boredom with the designated food sets in — even when the amounts are unlimited!

It's dinner on Day 7 and you have the "pleasure" of eating "all of the liver, papaya and lima beans your heart desires!" But, unfortunately, the last thing in the world you "desire" is liver, papaya and lima beans. Because during the past week you have consumed so much of those foods in every non-fattening form known to man, that the thought now makes your stomach growl and taste buds cringe!

DIETING FAILURE REASON #8

Dieters' willpowers wane as their hunger grows!

Let's face it! It's almost impossible *not* to eat when you are starving!

For instance ...

You've been invited to your best friend's birthday dinner — which just happens to fall on Day 6 of your diet when you are slated to have a head of raw cabbage and five kumquat for supper. Now what are you going to do?! Say to heck with dieting and join in? Or eat your cabbage and kumquat beforehand and then stalwartly sit and watch your companions indulge in succulent food and celebratory champagne; whilst you sip sanctimoniously on your personal bubbly (Club Soda, of course) ... only to find yourself sprawled in front of the television later that evening, salivating uncontrollably as the food commercials parade unmercifully before you?

By then, delirious with hunger (and faced with the revolting prospect of your next "meal" — "Cabbage Soup ... All you can slurp!"), you march straight to the kitchen and attack anything edible you can lay your hands on!

DIETING FAILURE REASON #9

Dieters are unable to live the rest of their lives on the diet that made them thin in the first place.

Why lose weight by fasting/ consuming only Chef's Salads/ drinking liquid protein/ or _____ *if* you are incapable of eating that way on a regular basis for the rest of your life?!

Sure, in moments of utter disgust, we dogmatically vow to diet "forever." In moments of utter frustration, we blindly think it boils down to a matter of willpower. But just how realistic are we being? I mean in all honesty, how many of us are able to survive a foodless vacuum of *just two weeks* (fourteen "short" days), let alone a lifetime?!

DIETING FAILURE REASON #10

Dieters succumb to the taste of food.

As Megan puts it, "I'm addicted to food, Pauline! I can't help myself. When food tastes good, I can't resist. *I simply can't stop eating*!"

Now, let's meet someone who *can* stop eating ... for a while, at least!

IF YOU WANT TO LOSE WEIGHT ... FILE FOR DIVORCE, FALL IN LOVE, OR FLY TO A REUNION!

Edith, a fellow tennis player, is truly one of the most stimulating, engaging people you could ever hope to meet! She is also a grandmother in her early sixties, who has a tummy not uncommon for women her age. In an attempt to get rid of "it," Edith yo-yos on and off a restrictive weight loss program monitored by daily weigh-ins.

Now Edith's motivation, like so many of us, is to lose weight for "something." Her upcoming Caribbean cruise. Her granddaughter's wedding. Her husband's retirement party. You name it, and Edith diets towards it. But while the events differ, the overall result does not. For no matter how dedicated she is to weight watching, Edith always ends up looking the same —

attractive, active and full of joie de vivre … with a tennis racquet in one hand, a carrot stick in the other, and a few extra pounds around her middle!

 FOOD FOR THOUGHT

Will you still be hooked on dieting when you are sixty-four?!

AFTER THE FAT

How many people do you know who have shed those unwanted pounds for a special occasion only to regain them after the event has come and gone?

I can think of many besides Edith.

There's Shirley (one of "those" heavier girls with "such a pretty face") who lost over *fifty* pounds for a big family reunion. In anxious expectation of the momentous event, she dieted with a passion; weighing and measuring every ounce of food. And her sacrifice and hard work were duly rewarded as she dropped pound after ugly pound. When the weekend of the reunion arrived, she truly looked gorgeous and slim. And as she visited with family members, Shirley glowed with pride as her equally proud husband beamed by her side! However, one year after the fat, Shirley was *sixty-five* pounds heavier!

My girlfriend, Sondra (another one of "those" women with a "such a pretty face"), dieted faithfully to be svelte for her wedding day. And on that appointed afternoon as she happily exchanged her wedding vows, she indeed looked characteristically beautiful and … uncharacteristically slim. In fact, she was thinner than I had ever seen her before (including high school!). But alas, her slenderness, too, was short-lived. For afterwards, Sondra packed on *all* of the lost pounds, **and then some**!

FOOD FOR THOUGHT

Why is it that so many of us diet successfully towards "something" (a wedding, a holiday, a reunion, a goal weight) only to predictably balloon up again?

This all too common phenomenon provides *the* most valuable insight of all into why dieters fail ...

DIETING FAILURE REASON #11

Dieters do not make a significant permanent change in their eating habits.

Unfortunately, diets are incorrectly perceived and utilized as *temporary* tools. And therein lies the problem. People embark upon a diet buoyed by the knowledge that they only have "x" number of pounds/weeks/ days/ hours to go before they can call it quits. Thus, once their goal is reached, they ironically go back to eating those foods, in those amounts that got them "fat" in the first place! (And we wonder why the weight returns!)

 FOOD FOR THOUGHT

In essence, when we go "on" a diet, we are basically setting ourselves up for failure.

Because in order for a diet (whatever form it takes) to be permanently effective, we must live with and "on" it for the rest of our lives ... forever and forever ... until death do us part!

(Get the picture?!)

85

FINAL FOOD FOR THOUGHT ON DIETS AND DIETING

As a diet veteran who has weathered years of mind-racking and stomach-growling dietitis, I finally realized that dieting doesn't work. Let's take one final look at the reasons for this before we move on to the next chapter.

THE PITFALLS OF DIETING

1) Dieters overeat after the denial and deprivation of dieting.

2) Dieters unintentionally force their metabolisms to become more energy efficient and "famine" sensitive.

3) Dieters refuse to accept their genetically predetermined, set-in-cement body stamps.

4) Dieters can not withstand the neverending stream of temptation that surrounds them.

5) Dieters set unrealistic goals.

6) Dieters feel ill (especially on unbalanced diets).

7) Dieters grow bored with the monotonous selection of designated food.

8) Dieters become certifiably hungry.

9) Dieters are unable to live the rest of their lives on the diet that made them thin in the first place.

10) Dieters succumb to the taste of food.

11) Dieters do not make a significant *permanent* change in their eating habits ... and therein lies **the ultimate crux of the matter!**

In our zeal to be slimmer, too many of us want to believe that a two week diet is the magical solution to all of our weight problems. Too many of us want to believe that one final round of deprivation will make us thin forever! ... ***But it won't!***

However, that's not what we want to hear. That's not what we choose to accept! On the contrary, we cling desperately to the notion that we can go on a diet; lose weight; and then go back to eating whatever we wish in the quantities we desire without ever having to confront our weight again. ***And we can't***, damn it!

Consequently, we diet over and over again, inflicting multiple waves of physical and emotional stress upon ourselves. Which brings us to the psychological and physiological ramifications of dieting. Two negative, pervading facets of The Dieting Game that end up intangibly beside the carrot and celery sticks on the plate of a chronic dieter.

Chapter 7

The Psychological and Physiological Ramifications of Dieting

THE PSYCHOLOGICAL RAMIFICATIONS OF DIETING

THE NUMBERS GAME

Over lunch one afternoon, the topic of conversation between Donna and I turned to (what else?) weight and dieting. Just as we were about to tuck into our Spinach Salads, Donna sighed; put down her fork, looked me straight in the eye, and said, "I try, you know, Pauline. I really do. I constantly watch every calorie I consume, but — [and this look of utter resignation filled her face] I still can't get down to my 'skinny' weight of March 17, 1986 when I was seventeen and three quarter pounds thinner at 142 1/4."

 FOOD FOR THOUGHT

Isn't it incredible how people who are caught up in dietitis can actually recite when they were their skinniest?!

And isn't it also incredible that although they were this "magical" weight for a relative instant; that number on the scale becomes their ideal poundage, and one to which they are constantly dieting to reattain?

Why are we so obsessed with those numbers on the scale? And what does this obsession do to us?

Let's take a closer look.

DOESN'T ALMOST EVERY WOMAN YOU KNOW WANT TO BE AT LEAST FIVE POUNDS THINNER?!

Anne, Carol, Jackie and I were sitting on Anne's patio enjoying diet lemonade and fresh fruit one beautiful spring morning following a vigorous ladies double's match. After the usual tennis chatter (where each point is replayed ten times over!), I practically choked on my cantaloupe when Jackie (who has the dynamite figure we all envy!) started complaining about her weight.

To which Carol replied in visible astonishment, "I can't believe it! I've always thought that you have one of the best bodies of any women I know! And my husband thinks so, too!"

And thus, a two and a half hour discussion ensued about weight, women and dieting, during which time Jackie confessed that her life was dominated by the bathroom scale.

She confided, "I'm currently at my *top weight* ... five pounds above my normal weight and ten pounds above where I really feel thin." (Sound familiar? I mean, ideally don't all of us want to be five pounds thinner than our skinniest weight, so that we have a five pound leeway?!)

Jackie ended the conversation by saying she was simply *delighted* because her husband was leaving the next day on a three week business trip, and she was going to eat salads the entire time he was gone!

And I was left flabbergasted to discover that someone who had such a perfect figure *thought* she was fat, and was heavily into the Numbers Game! It just didn't add up!

PERHAPS STEPHANIE'S BODY IS TRYING TO TELL HER SOMETHING!

Stephanie is another person who insists on playing Bathroom Scale Roulette. Like many women, Stephanie is not fat, but she "thinks" she is. As a result, she constantly complains about being ten pounds overweight, and frets and diets endlessly over those "extra" pounds. When listening to her one day, I thought to myself, "Isn't there a lesson to be learned here, albeit, a very frustrating one?…

Perhaps Stephanie's body is trying to tell her something. Perhaps it is trying to say it doesn't want/ have/ need to be ten pounds thinner!"

 FOOD FOR THOUGHT

By stopping and listening to their bodies and accepting them for what they are, people like Stephanie, Jackie and Donna have the opportunity to become happier, healthier individuals.

Because there is so much more to life than hopping on and off the scales; worrying non-stop about those stupid five/ ten/ _____ pounds that keep being lost and regained over and over again! Not only is it a complete waste of time and energy, but it is also incredibly emotionally exhausting!

I should know.

You see, for many years my life was heavily weighted down by that small piece of bathroom furniture. In fact, I still have haunting memories of my mandatory morning weigh-ins.

90

ISN'T IT STRANGE, HOW THAT TINY NEEDLE ON THAT LITTLE BATHROOM SCALE CAN MAKE OR BREAK OUR HAPPINESS FOR THE DAY?!

The very first duty I performed upon awakening every day was to go to the bathroom. After that, I would fiddle with the adjustor knob on the scale to ensure that the needle was positioned precisely at zero, and not a fraction over! Next, I'd strip stark naked (even shedding my rings, for heaven's sake!) to step ever so gingerly onto the scale, in hopes of coaxing it not to register an ounce heavier. Then I'd record the weight in my mind, step off, and again peer down at that stupid little needle to see if it rebounded exactly to zero. If it didn't (if it rested even a hair breadth over — or if I was unhappy with the result!), I'd repeat the whole neurotic process again!

Isn't it strange how that slender needle on that almighty bathroom scale can make or break our happiness for the day?! … If we are lighter after our morning ritual, an uncontrollable euphoria pulses throughout our ecstatic skinnier being! We hop off the scale ready to face the challenges of our weight watching day with head held high and a successful spring in our step. The needle has buoyed our spirits, and we feel strong and rejuvenated in our "battle" against the bulge. This time, we are going to be skinny *once and for all*!

We can say an emphatic "No!" to those freshly baked Cinnamon Buns on our coffee break. We can chomp our celery and carrot sticks with even greater conviction at lunch! The positive reinforcement provided by the weight of the needle on the scale that morning has served to further strengthen our determination to succeed, and to make this *the* "diet to end all of our diets."

Furthermore, we carry a song in our heart as we happily trot off to aerobics where we more enthusiastically than ever perform our donkey kicks and fire hydrants. With each drop of sweat we gleefully admonish, "Take that you flabby thigh — I'm getting rid of you once and for all!" And as we lay in bed that night falling asleep to the sounds of our rumbling stomach, we feel a smug sense of starved satisfaction. *We are succeeding!* Nothing can stop us now!

Thus, early the next day, we step onto the scales overflowing with confident anticipation. We were so "good" yesterday. We didn't cheat even one little sliverful ... *and* we exercised like a Jane Fonda look-alike. We are bright-eyed with the belief that the ruling will be in our favor. The judge will certainly pound the weight of his gavel even further to the left of yesterday!

We look down assuredly expectant. But ...

"Oh no! It can't be true."

The needle points decisively, derisively to a full pound heavier!

As the realization sinks in, a gnawing feeling forms in the pit of our empty stomach and races up to our deflated, stunned psyche. How can we tackle another day of constant denial? Another day of carrot and celery sticks? Another night of falling asleep to the unanswered demands of our growling stomach?

Throughout the morning we keep shaking our head in disbelief as we repeatedly mutter, "I gained weight! Why?"

"Am I about to start my period? Am I retaining water? ... Why, oh why, did I gain that stupid pound?"

Over and over ... again and again, we anxiously question, "**Why**?!?"

And at lunch, being perplexed, frustrated, and demoralized over gaining that one earth-shattering pound, we consume (in hurt defiance) a Chocolate Milk Shake, a Deluxe Bacon Cheeseburger, and a jumbo side of fries. Bloated, burping, and laden with guilt (not to mention food!), we waddle out of the restaurant feeling physically ill (we are so stuffed), and mentally unhinged (we have failed — *again*!).

Then, after stewing all afternoon over our eating trespasses, we somehow end up in the kitchen where we attack an unfinished box of Oreos, or whatever else we can lay our hands on. Now we are really furious with ourselves and more miserable than ever! We hate the thought of going to aerobics, but know we should. Once there, we drag ourselves half-heartedly through our "punishment," with every pound of jiggling fat repulsively reminding us of our failure. Just yesterday we felt sleek and svelte in our leotards; today we feel like The Human Blob personified!

And what is the first thing we do the following morning (after, of course, we resolve to embark upon yet another diet)? That's right, we hop right back onto those stupid scales to see where that needle will fall — once again placing ourselves at the command of our merciless demigod!

IT'S A BITCH!!

My naturally thin friend Denise is extremely understanding of the emotional rigors that beset dieters (bless her skinny soul!). Almost guiltily she admits, "Pauline, I look at people who are trying to lose weight and my heart goes out to them. I love food so much. It must be terrible to have to constantly say '*no*' and be worried about what you're eating all the time."

It is, Denise.

Speaking from experience, I can tell you that, simply put ... *dieting is a bitch*!

Words can not convey just how frustrating, demoralizing and anxiety-ridden food deprivation can be!

But unlike Denise, most naturally thin people are not as empathetic towards those who are heavy; much less to the emotional hell that dieting entails. I mean, haven't we all witnessed someone slim disdainfully eyeing a fat person and commenting, "Why doesn't she '*do something*' about herself? Where's her self-respect? You'd think she could exert some willpower and go on a diet?!"

Ah, that omnipotent word "willpower." If only fat people got mentally tougher and practiced more self-control, they wouldn't be such slobs, right?

Not necessarily!

With megaovereaters aside, many heavier people *do* exert willpower, and plenty of it! Like Natasha, who sipped water throughout a succulent Prime Rib dinner in celebration of her husband's birthday because she was in the middle of a liquid protein diet! *And that isn't willpower*?

I, too, can remember countless times of deprivation. One being when I dined at the Burger King with a group of friends; only to watch them tuck into their Big Whoppers whilst I gnawed righteously (but admittedly, enviously) on a carrot stick the size of a baseball bat. Why? The next day was my final weigh-in for the diet contest at work!

HOW MUCH WILLPOWER DOES ONE HAVE TO POSSESS AND FOR HOW LONG?

Now some critics might argue that fat people may have the willpower to diet, but they simply do not have the intestinal fortitude to sustain it. In other words, the big problem with "fatties" is that they are unable to stick with a diet over the long haul. However ...

What about someone like Evelyn who dieted for *an entire year* and lost over one hundred pounds?! Although she eventually regained the weight, didn't she demonstrate an **unbelievable** amount of willpower for an **extraordinary** length of time?

 FOOD FOR THOUGHT

Just how much willpower does one have to possess and for how long before it is enough?

A lifetime ...?

94

WHEN THE RIGOURS OF DIETING BECOME TOO MUCH TO BEAR

Unfortunately, dieters are not superhuman. Unfortunately, it is impossible for any individual to perpetually deny themselves the pleasure of food, regardless of how badly they want to lose weight. Because underlying everything is the tormenting agony and isolation that accompanies perpetual denial. Seeing others enjoy Big Macs, Kentucky Fried Chicken, and Banana Splits is enough to drive even the most well-intentioned dieter crazy!

So what happens when the rigors of dieting become too much to bear?... We break down and cheat! And what does cheating accomplish? Why, it only serves to heighten our anguish even further! Because then we have the mental consequences of our "crime" to face. A self-imposed trial takes place, usually as our body is trying to achingly digest the "evidence."

"What's the matter with me ... (burp)? Why can't I be stronger? I'm just a fat slob who has absolutely no (hiccup) willpower."

Verdict?! ... Guilty, as charged!

Sentence?! ... The latest diet!!

OUR FAT IS HANGING OUT FOR ALL THE WORLD TO SEE

But, we eventually become so fed up with constantly weight watching and worrying that we decide to eat what we want and enjoy ourselves. "What the heck," we rationalize, "dieting doesn't seem to make a difference anyway. All I do is lose weight and gain it back again. So, why bother?"

However, when we choose not to diet, we end up replacing one source of stress for another. Because while we may relish what we are eating at the time, we are unhappy with ourselves after the act. The truth of the "fatter" is that we don't want to be a size 14/ 16/ 18/ _____ (you fill in the number). We don't want to be sausaged into our jeans only to have the seam lines etched into the tops of our legs and our zippers digging into our belly buttons. We don't want to spend the rest of our lives fat and miserable!

Thus, all of these conflicting feelings build up into a whistling kettle-full of emotions ready to boil over. And added to the pressure of this personal frustration, is the public humiliation of knowing that our fat is hanging out for all the world to see — and condemn. Because fatness is afforded no privacy; past dieting attempts given no credit. As a result, heavier people are left unprotected prey to the negative and demeaning attitudes of a glossy cover girl society. A society that judges beauty in the form of pounds and inches, with little regard for the weight of an individual's heart and soul.

 FOOD FOR THOUGHT

When you really think about it, dieters are truly amazing because:

Despite the continual frustration they harbour over their weight.

Despite all of the anxiety, stress and denial associated with dieting.

Despite the formidable social pressure that exists in our food-filled, thin-is-in society.

And, despite the fact they repeatedly end up fat again virtually overnight ...

Dieters are willing to wake up to yet one more Monday morning of deprivation!

 **FINAL FOOD FOR THOUGHT ON THE PSYCHOLOGICAL RAMIFICATIONS OF DIETING**

ROUND AND ROUND IT GOES ... AND WHEN WILL IT STOP?!

As far as our bodies and weight are concerned, most of us want desperately to be able "to have our cake *and* eat it, too." We simply want to eat what we wish and be thin at the same time. Therefore, we are worriedly unhappy when dieting *and* worriedly unhappy when we are not. On the one hand, we think we should be "doing something" to get rid of our fat, and see no alternative but to go on another diet. However, on the other, we dread the deprivation it brings. So, *we eat*, then we worry about it. Then *we diet,* and we worry about it. We break our diet, and we worry about that. So, we go back on a diet, and we worry again!

Diet, diet, diet; **worry, worry, worry**; *eat, eat, eat*; **worry, worry, worry**; *diet, diet, diet*; **worry**, *eat, diet,* **worry**. Round and round it goes ... And when will it end? How can we break this cycle of mental anguish and frustration?

Well, one thing's for sure — we can't stop eating! Unlike an alcoholic or drug addict who can practice total abstention, we don't have that option!

Thus, an ongoing war rages between ourselves and food. A war waged on many different fronts and known by many different names: The Starve/Binge Cycle, The Yo-Yo Syndrome, Dieter's Dilemma, Carbs vs. Cals. The name doesn't really matter. It's you, the casualty, who needs to regroup and attack the situation if you are ultimately going to win the battle of your bulge!

THE TURNING POINT

In my relentless pursuit of thinness, my world became heavily overshadowed by the dark oppressive storm clouds of dieting. And as the grooves of worry about what I ate and how much I weighed penetrated further into my mind, I could feel my life being overtaken. And then something occurred that became the catalyst for my self-actualization. Something that finally enabled me put my body and food into proper perspective. Although the event did not immediately alter my perceptions; in retrospect, "it" was the turning point — the mitigating circumstance that channeled me in the direction of normalizing relations with my body!

Here's what happened.

THE PHYSIOLOGICAL RAMIFICATIONS OF DIETING
A MOST DANGEROUS GAME

It was early April, and five months after my three short-lived visits to the psychiatrist. Summer was fast approaching, and several people at work had organized a diet contest where each participant put seventy-five dollars into a kitty and then officially weighed in on the Detecto scale at the doctor's office next door. Six weeks later, the person who lost the greatest percentage of body weight would win the contest and the cash.

After some serious introspection, I decided to throw my money and fat into the ring for two reasons. First, I was not enjoying my new job and had packed on a few pounds out of sheer frustration. And second, I knew a stressful time lay ahead of me, as I was quitting in hopes of securing a teaching position that fall. Therefore, rather than eat out of anxiety and uncertainty, I decided to place all of my energies into losing weight. After all, what if I didn't get a teaching assignment, *and* I gained weight in the meantime — double depression, and most likely, double the weight gain!

Well, my competitive spirit came through and I dieted with a passion. I ate (if you could call it eating!) like a bird; and exercised daily like an Olympic athlete. I remember having a horrific cold and losing my taste buds for two weeks — everything tasted like cardboard, and I couldn't have been more delighted! I also recall eating two huge carrots and three thin rye crisps the day before the final weigh-in. I was psyched! I was going to win, *and* I was going to be thin forever!

I came in second. Richard beat me (those darn men can always lose weight quicker!) … *but*, I was one hundred and seventy-five dollars richer (second prize), fourteen and a half pounds lighter; and to top everything off, the teaching job was mine! I was flying high! Until, of course, I started to regain the weight. Once I stopped existing on carrot sticks and rye crisps, the pounds promptly returned!

Six months later (and in the middle of yet another self-imposed starvation regime), my doctor encouraged me to take a break from the pill. And as a result, something troubling came to light … I had "lost" my period! Dieting and exercising to such extremes over such a long time, had eventually taken its physical toll! I had tampered with the intricate and sensitive workings of my body one too many times — and I was finally paying the price!

 FOOD FOR THOUGHT

In our quest to be outwardly slim and beautiful, we often seriously neglect and abuse ourselves within. Not once did I think about the inner harm my repetitive dieting might cause, until that fateful day when I learned I had lost my period. In the meantime, I awaited anxiously for its return — not knowing when, or if, it would.

Fortunately, it arrived a year later. And along with it came a dawning realization that marked the beginning of the peace I would eventually make in the war I had been waging against my poor defenseless body. I began to see my physical self in a different light. I began to appreciate and respect my body. I began to realize what a dangerous game I had been playing.

BEARING A CHILD

My subsequent pregnancy further reinforced my deepening bodily respect and appreciation. During those nine months, the crucial involuntary actions orchestrated from within (and completely beyond my physical and intellectual control) were simply mind-boggling! For example, while Ryan was developing inside of me, I was not aware of the exact moment his heart started beating, or when his eyes began forming. Once conception took place, my body was a home for my baby, but — I was not in command of the multitude of miracles that were taking place. Apart from trying to live as healthy a lifestyle as possible, everything else was out of my immediate control.

Similarly, I did not initiate the commencement of contractions that brought Ryan forth into the world. His arrival was not precipitated by my blowing a whistle and saying, "Okay, bod, now's the time to get that oxytocin rolling!" On the contrary, my body stepped in and just did what had to be done. I consciously assisted with the drug-free birth, but basically my body was in the driver's seat and I was its passenger. My physical being had taken things into its own hands and was working conscientiously and diligently on my behalf!

 FOOD FOR THOUGHT

Pregnancy and childbirth made me stop and consider the myriad of inner operations that our bodies miraculously perform! While we are busy living our lives, our physical plants are quietly and incredulously humming away behind the scenes to sustain our survival.

And what fuel is required for this wonderful machine to function properly?

Water and a balanced diet.

But what do we so frequently supply it with?

Insufficient and unnutritious food!

100

A CALORIC DALLIANCE WITH A BANANA SPLIT

It's difficult, isn't it, to conceptualize food's primary function by extending our perception of it past our lips and hips into the realm of its important chemical interplay within our bodies?

For example ...

When we order a Banana Split, we do so to satisfy our taste buds — not our daily nutritional requirements. As our spoon sinks into that succulent sweetness and our tongue follow suit, how many of us are consciously contemplating what the calcium in the ice cream and the potassium in the banana will do for our body? The truth is, we are more concerned about the impact our caloric dalliance with that Banana Split will have upon our stomach/ hips/ derriere, and not upon our bodily functions!

Furthermore, when we go on a fad diet, how many of us think about the physiological consequences? For in reality, if we consume too little food or restrict ourselves to only certain foods, we rob our body of essential vitamins and minerals ... vitamins and minerals that are responsible for a multitude of life-sustaining biological processes. Like cell multiplication, regulation of blood glucose levels, growth and repair of tissues, transmission of nerve impulses, transportation of oxygen, conversion of fatty and amino acids, and the synthesis of DNA and RNA ... just to mention a few! (It's almost scary, isn't it?)

 FINAL FOOD FOR THOUGHT ON THE PHYSIOLOGICAL RAMIFICATIONS OF DIETING

Those of us who flit from one diet and weight to another inadvertently wreak havoc upon our physical plants. In essence, we throw our bodies into a confused state of metabolic flux by forcing them to cope with the onerous task of working optimally without enough nutrients one week; and being deluged with them the next. Furthermore, we may delight in our slimmer waistline as a result of existing on pineapple and papaya for fourteen "short" days, but what is the physical price to be paid?

Sadly, it's not until we lose our period, or our hair ... it's not until the inner damage we inflict upon ourselves becomes outwardly visible, that we consider the chemical relationship between our bodies and food — *and* — how repetitive dieting interferes with the normal functioning of a healthy human body.

Unfortunately, as chronic dieters, we choose to remain blind to the negative ramifications of dieting until we see some obvious, irrefutable repercussion. Unfortunately, our major concern is to be thin and beautiful at all costs — physical and emotional!

Chapter 8

Exercise

I love how I *feel* following a challenging tennis match! I love how I *feel* after walking around the Stanley Park seawall! I love how I *feel* as I luxuriate in the hot tub after swimming laps! In essence, I love exercising because it makes me *feel* physically cleansed and emotionally empowered to be the best I can be!

How do you feel about exercise?

Has it become a horrible chore … a 6 a.m. wake up call to drag yourself to an early bird aerobic's class? A source of embarrassment because you feel too fat to exercise? An addiction, fueled by the frenetic desire to transform your body into that of a supermodel?

If so, exercise doesn't have to be that way. In fact, it musn't! On the contrary, exercise should elicit warm, positive feelings that uplift your spirits and make you feel good inside and out!

Unfortunately, however, we often allow the size and shape of our body to stand as a barrier between ourselves and a happy, prosperous relationship with exercise, don't we?

I should know.

For although I have always loved how exercise makes me feel, I have also been guilty of exercising for the wrong reasons … to reshape my body; to rid myself of excess calories; and to divest myself of guilt, shame, and bodily dissatisfaction.

PUSHUPS FOR THE MIND!

Have you ever stopped to consider the emotional roadblocks that prevent you from having a healthy relationship with exercise?

Hold onto that thought as we run through this chapter, taking a closer look at some of the major exercise hurdles we erect!

IF I ONLY LOOKED BETTER IN A BATHING SUIT!

Elva laments, "If only I wasn't so fat *then* I would definitely join a fitness club. But ... whenever I muster up enough courage to go out and do something about my body, I find myself surrounded by women who look as if they have just slipped off the front cover of *VOGUE* magazine. And then I feel so humiliated and disgusted with myself, that all I want to do is run home and (perverse as it may sound) seek comfort in food!"

 PUSHUPS FOR THE MIND!

Isn't there an "Elva" in each of us?

I mean, aren't we all self-conscious about our bodies in some "weigh," shape or form? (Remember Christie Brinkley and her "big" hips?!)

But ...

Regardless of how embarrassed we are, or how fat we feel, we must overcome those negative, self-deprecating feelings and say,

"I am going to exercise! Because regular exercise is essential to my physical and emotional well-being. Furthermore, I only have one life to live and one body to live it in. And to be the best

I can possibly be bodywise and healthwise, I need to cast aside my self-consciousness/ laziness/ low self-esteem/ _____ and make exercise a natural part of my life, a habit like brushing my teeth."

However, in order to accomplish this. In order to exercise on a regular and permanent basis, it is absolutely imperative that you *choose an activity you truly enjoy and can stick with over time*!

In light of this, don't be deterred if you are unathletic or "allergic" to unnecessary movement! Because there has got to be one physical activity that appeals to you. Take walking, for example, it's a perfect exercise that is easy on the mind and "soles!"

For example, walking doesn't demand special skills or super-human amounts of physical exertion. Nor does it require intricate scheduling, expensive equipment, or embarrassing hiphugging outfits (like bathing suits and spandex tights). In fact, all you have to do is throw on something roomy like a loose pair of pants; lace up your shoes; and step out the door ... to walk quickly, slowly; a short distance, long distance; rain or shine; during the day or night; on your own, with a pet, a neighbour, a friend.

What could be simpler or easier?

And that's the beauty of walking. It is a pleasant, stress-free activity that affords you the luxury and convenience of setting your own time, place, pace, and distance! Therefore, if you're like Elva and extremely self-conscious and publicly ashamed of your body, you can walk under the cover of darkness or a baggy coat! If you are a stay-at-home parent, you can walk the kids to and from school, or take the baby out in the buggy for a daily spin around the block. If you ride public transit, you can disembark before your scheduled stop and walk to your destination. Again, the choice is yours; the options unlimited! And because of this, because walking is so easy to do and so easy to fit into your lifestyle, it makes it easy for you to get out there and "just do it!" on a regular basis.

And therein lies the heart of the matter.

 PUSHUPS FOR THE MIND!

The benefits of exercise are cumulative. Therefore, small caloric expenditures are like compound interest — over the long term a little ends up steadily becoming a lot!

And that's the key — the real pay off comes when you exercise regularly and moderately **over the long term**.

Because in reality, the number of calories burned during physical activity is negligible on a per time basis (i.e. twelve minutes of running will only work off the equivalent of one medium apple, or one small bran muffin — without butter!). *However*, when accumulated over time, small caloric expenditures are worth their weight in gold. Thus, you may have to walk nine miles to lose one measly pound ... but walking half an hour, three times a week for a year, will leave ten solid pounds lying in the dust! And that's nothing to sneeze at!

So you see, exercise *does not have to be* (and should not be!) an arduous "blood, sweat and tears" production. Because the truth is you don't have to exercise with the intensity and commitment of an Olympic athlete in order for your workout to be beneficial. You don't have to be like Lois, for example, who feels compelled to work out every day (sometimes more than once depending upon how much she has eaten)! **All you have to do is exercise 3 times a week for a minimum 20 minutes per session.**

With that in mind, contemplate this.

WHIPLASHED

For the past three years, I have been sidelined with a severe whiplash injury that has seriously circumscribed my life and curtailed my physical activity. Where I once was an extremely active person who exercised almost daily, my activity level since the accident has been limited to swimming twenty minutes three times a week and walking occasionally. Have I gained weight? Would you believe … no! In fact, my weight has remained exactly the same — without the self-inflicted torture of a tyrannical exercise regime!

So what does this tell us?

It tells us that we do not have to exercise neurotically to reap the benefits. All we need to do is exercise moderately on a steady basis (a minimum 20 minutes, 3 times a week!). And then if we end up doing more, it's a bonus!

And besides, vowing to exercise excessively (intensely and every day, for example) only leads to failure and frustration. Why? Because we are making exercise promises that we (and our bodies) can't keep! I mean, regardless of our honourable intentions, how many of us are actually going to be able to devote the time and energy necessary to sustain a grueling activity level? Not to mention the fact that "something" inevitably happens (we get sick or the dog has puppies!) to prevent us from following through.

Believe me, over the long run, you are far better off to to set realistic goals that promote a healthy body and mind-set! Here's what can happen when you don't.

EXERCISING YOUR CALORIES AWAY

It was Christmas Eve 1979, and my husband and I were hosting a special Ukrainian Christmas Eve dinner for our families (a gathering of twenty-five people). Well, can you believe that amidst the last minute flurry of food preparation, housework, and gift buying, I actually squeezed in a jog? Then after dinner, I literally left my astonished guests at the table, grabbed my Nikes and went for a run! Only to awaken early the next morning (Christmas Day!) to don my track suit once again. Why?

I felt compelled to "work out" in order to "work off" what I had eaten.

 PUSHUPS FOR THE MIND!

There is no doubt that exercise is invaluable in terms of balancing caloric input and output. And as such, it only makes sense to gauge the amount of food you eat against the amount of exercise you do.

However...

It is virtually impossible to work off all of the calories you consume normally (let alone those incurred through binging!). Furthermore, there is a fine line between exercising as a natural part of a healthful lifestyle, and exercising obsessively to burn off what you have eaten.

But my problem lay deeper than that. For not only did I exercise to divest myself of calories; but as each foot pounded the pavement, I also truly and naively believed that "penance" for my overeating "sins" was being served.

 DOUBLE TIME PUSHUPS FOR THE MIND!

No exercise program should be bound by feelings of guilt and shame. Because the bizarre punishment and reward system associated with those unproductive emotions, only serves to negate the true uplifting value of exercise. In addition, your motive for working out

must not be attached to the erroneous belief that when you exercise you are "doing something" about your fat hips/ legs/ _____. Conversely, when you don't exercise, you "deserve" to have them.

Oh no.

Your motivation to exercise should be for the health of it! ... To be the very best you can possibly be physically and emotionally within the body you've got — regardless of your size and shape.

Jog on the spot with that, as you digest this.

WHY DO YOU HAVE TO EXERCISE, YOU'RE NOT EVEN FAT!

At a ladies' clothing party one evening, the topic of conversation turned to (what else?!) bodily dissatis"fat"tion. Eva started the ball rolling by wistfully declining Nancy's Magic Bars with, "Geez, I'd like to, but ...!" She then explained, "I'm sick and tired of being fat. I started the 'Sunshine Diet' on Monday, [when else?] and I've vowed to exercise every day!"

Then the dam burst and everyone chimed in with their personal weight problems. However, conversation ground to a screeching halt when Rita, a certifiable bonerack, added that she felt flabby and needed to exercise. Sheila turned to her and voiced aloud what all of us were thinking, "For heaven's sakes, Rita, why do you have to exercise? ... *You're not even fat*!?!"

 PUSHUPS FOR THE MIND!

Isn't it strange how we naturally assume that because someone is thin, they don't need to exercise?

*And isn't it sad that we are so conditioned to believe
that a thin body is a beautiful body, we lose sight of
the fact that the true beauty of exercise goes beyond
our body measurements and into the realm of health
and physical fitness?*

Misconceptions such as these illustrate the need for us to understand that no matter what a person's size and shape, *everyone* should exercise — *be they fat, thin, or in between*! — because the physical and emotional rewards are simply too important to ignore!

Here's something else that is too important to ignore ... another barrier that prevents us from having a healthy relationship with exercise. One that is erected when bodily dissatisfaction is coupled with the unrealistic desire to attain a picture perfect body!

WE COULD RUN RINGS AROUND THE EQUATOR

Pamela proudly announced the other day that she had bounced her way through Jane Fonda's Workout Challenge **three** times *in the last twelve hours*! (That's a total of four and half hour's worth of *very* strenuous exercise!) She proceeded to say, "I hate my big, fat, ugly thunder thighs, Pauline, and I am bound and determined to get rid of them once and for all. You know how it is."

I smiled in polite reply, but inwardly shuddered. I knew exactly what she meant. For I have been where she is at!

You see, as P.E. teacher I am acutely aware of the importance of exercise to our physical and emotional well-being. However, prior to developing a healthy relationship with exercise, a part of me (the well-indoctrinated product of our thin-obsessed society) held steadfast to the mistaken belief that the perfect figure lay just at the end of the next lap or aerobic's class.

But fortunately I now know differently.

Fortunately, after one too many fitness classes, pool lengths, and track laps, I finally realized that exercise can not convert a body into a size and shape it wasn't meant to be. Consequently, Pamela and I could spend the rest of our lives running rings around the equator, **but** ... she will never succeed in exercising her shorter, stockier legs into the gazelle-like limbs of super-model; and I will never succeed in having a Playboy Playmate's bum.

But I accept that now, and you must, too!

 PUSHUPS FOR THE MIND!

> *As difficult and unsettling as it may be, you must let go of the belief that if you exercise long and hard enough, you will eventually look like a Jane Fonda, Cindy Crawford, or Kathy Smith. Because that is a physical impossibility!*

However ...

> *It is physically possible to have the best body you can own and be in the best possible shape you can be, by exercising on a moderate, regular basis!*

Again, the key words are **moderate** and **regular**. Because more is not better as far as exercise is concerned. I'm living proof of that. In fact, my body doesn't look any different or shapelier now than it did when I neurotically overexercised, **but** my attitude has changed dramatically. You see, today I exercise for all the right reasons. Today, I exercise without the guilt and disappointment of unmet unrealistic expectations! And I couldn't be happier or feel better!

FINAL PUSHUPS FOR THE MIND!

I began this chapter by saying I love the way exercise makes me feel. I began this book by saying it doesn't matter how much I exercise, I know I will always have bigger hips in proportion to the rest of my body. Unfortunately, it took years of blood, sweat and tears before I was able to reconcile these two concepts in my mind. And in the process, I learned this (the hard way!) ...

Exercise does provide figure shaping rewards! Exercise does burn calories. Exercise does tone muscles! Exercise does aid in weight loss! *However* ... exercise, like dieting, is not a magic panacea, a "quick fix" that automatically grants the participant a perfect body or absolves them of their overeating "sins."

And once I got that through my head, I began to exercise for the health of it ... to be the very best I can be physically and emotionally within the god-given body I've got!

And you must do the same!

You must select an activity you enjoy and then go for the gusto! And in the process, pamper yourself a little. Find a pool with a hot tub. Make a regular date to go for a walk with a friend and then do lunch. Treat yourself to a facial or manicure after a workout!

Go ahead! The rewards are priceless! And you and your body couldn't be more worth it!

Chapter 9

Abnormal Eating

HELP! IS THERE ANYONE ELSE OUT THERE WHO PICKS AT THE RAISINS UNDERNEATH THE BANANA BREAD?!

Picture this.

A friend is dropping by this afternoon, so you have whipped up a batch of prize-winning Chewy, Chewy Chocolate Chip Pecan Dream Cookies. However, in the process (shudder!), you have spooned gobfuls of cookie dough into your mouth. Hence, at the appointed hour you find yourself burping, bloated and miserable ... unable to have a single cookie with your friend *like a normal human being*! because the sight of those stupid cookies makes you feel positively sick.

There you sit the entire time. Hating yourself. Secretly envying your thinner companion as you watch her carefully select, slowly eat, and thoroughly *enjoy* two cookies! There you sit. Silently seething and inwardly screaming, "*You idiot! Why did you have to bake those ?!!?! cookies anyway?*" And there you sit, uncomfortably awash in shame ... as you grit your teeth and vow dogmatically to start yet another diet at the crack of dawn tomorrow!

And horror of horrors, you feel so badly at having overeaten in such an abnormal manner, that you wake up in the middle of the night only to find yourself standing in the kitchen eating first one, and then another, after another of those stupid little cookies!

Half-asleep, you know you should stop eating, *but you can't*! ... until you are burping, bloated, and full of shame once again!

And as you trundle off to bed laden with guilt (not to mention cookies!), you resolutely start to reformulate tomorrow's diet. As you slip between the sheets and drift into sleep, the renewed conviction wells up inside of you. "I *will* start a new diet come the morning." (Burp!) "And this time, I *will* succeed!" (Hiccup.)

Thus, you awaken bright and early filled with the desire and determination to uphold your resolution. "This will be *the* 'diet to end all of my diets!' This time I'll reign supreme over my '*will*' power." ... "Oh yes, *this* time for sure!"

Which, of course, means eating nothing all day. Breakfast is easy to skip because, let's face it, you're still full from the night before! Lunch isn't a problem either. Except your frustration and disappointment are intensified as you watch *normal* people eat their *normal* lunches because they have a *normal* relationship with food. They aren't guilty of getting up in the middle of the night and devouring God knows how many Chewy, Chewy Chocolate Chip Pecan Dream Cookies!

Your real test, however, comes in the late afternoon; when ravenous, one of three situations predictably occurs. First, as soon as you walk through the door, the kitchen pulls you to its midst like a puppet on a string. Once there, you attack whatever food you can lay your hands on (eating far more than if you simply had a proper breakfast, lunch and dinner to begin with!).

Or second, you are able to contain your hunger until dinner time ... when, half-crazed with starvation, you wolf down a huge meal (again consuming more than if you had just eaten a normal breakfast, lunch and dinner).

Or third, continuing to be saint-like and full of willpower, you conscientiously partake of a Spartan dieter's supper. (You know the type well. Broiled this, weighed that. One orange and purple polka-dotted fruit from the X-rated column; one pink striped veggie from the Z ... Yuk! Thank God, my life is not subjected to that any more!) Then, buoyed by your successful day, you readjust your dieter's halo and head off to further punish your body at aerobics!

Thus, if you have been able to sanctimoniously starve and exercise your way this far into the evening, the next crucial touch-and-go time presents itself. Will you break down and move as if mesmerized to those remaining, surviving cookies? Those cookies that unmercifully attempt to sabotage your honorable intentions with seductive whispers of, *"Eat me! Eat me!"* (Heard by your ears only, of course!)

Or, with pursed lips will you stiffen your resolve and righteously retire? ... Only to find yourself (horror upon horrors!) standing in the middle of the kitchen in the middle of the night, chomping once again on those stupid Chewy, Chewy Chocolate Chip Pecan Dream Cookies! ... Only to awaken the next morning with the horrible realization of, *"Oh no!* I did it — *again!"* And thus the vicious cycle continues.

 FOOD FOR THOUGHT

"Once I start eating _____ (you fill in the culprit), I just can't seem to stop until I've eaten the whole thing ... or most of it!!"

BUT PAULINE, IF YOU LIKE PANCAKES ... WHY CAN'T YOU JUST HAVE ONE OR TWO?

I can vividly recall a conversation that took place during breakfast one morning with my sister-in-law Anne. I had just placed a stack of blueberry pancakes and a bottle of syrup in front of her, and was sitting down to a bowl of Cabbage Soup ... when she glanced at my food in surprise, and justifiably questioned, *"What, in heaven's name are you eating?"*

"Cabbage soup," I replied nonchalantly (trying to sound as if it was a common breakfast commodity!).

"Don't you like pancakes, Pauline?" she queried.

"Yes," I murmured somewhat sheepishly.

"Well, why don't you have some then?" Anne offered logically.

"I can't," I replied matter-of-factly, avoiding eye contact.

"But, Pauline," she persisted, "can't you just have one or two ... without the syrup?"

"No," I stated a little defensively (privately wishing that people would leave us dieters alone), *"I can't!"*

 FOOD FOR THOUGHT

"Once I start eating _____*, I just can't seem to stop until I've eaten the whole thing ... or most of it!!"*

I'M SORRY, PAULINE ... I CAN'T COME TO COME TO TEA TODAY!

One of my very favourite pastimes while living in Bangkok was to enjoy High Tea at the Regent. I grasped every opportunity to relax in that luxuriant hotel lobby ... listening to the string quartet whilst I sipped tea from fine china and nibbled upon a smorgasbord of afternoon delights. Thus, on the occasion of Rosemary's birthday, she and I had arranged to celebrate in this exquisite setting.

However, early the appointed day Rosemary phoned and greeted me with a despondent, "I'm sorry, Pauline ... but I can't come to tea today."

"Why not?" I queried, taken aback.

"Because," Rosemary explained dejectedly, "I'm thirty pounds overweight. *None* of my clothes fit anymore. And I am sick and tired of being fat! I hate myself. I am so confused ... I don't know what diet to go on next! And, the last place in the world I want to be is the Regent where I will be surrounded by all of that bloody food!"

FOOD FOR THOUGHT

Can you control yourself during a smorgasbord situation?

There was a time when I most certainly could not! In fact, before I normalized my relationship with food, I found smorgasbords *deadly*! There I would stand, plate in hand, salivating over the seemingly endless row of enticing culinary offerings, excited at the prospect of the tempting taste sensations that lay before me, but also harbouring these two disturbing thoughts.

One, if the buffet was at a restaurant, I felt I had to eat my money's worth. (What ludicrous logic! Because a smorgasbord costs the same whether you eat a lot or not, *but* the price your body pays differs immensely!) And two, because there was so much tantalizing food available, I felt that ...

Once I started eating ... *I just couldn't stop* until I was absolutely stuffed!

I CAN'T BAKE BECAUSE I'LL EAT IT

A group of us, all women, sat around Elizabeth's dining room table one winter's evening contemplating dessert (and our waistlines!) after a feast of Shrimp and Crab Newburg. We gazed with unbridled anticipation as our host then served the pièce de résistance — Death by Chocolate! — right before our drooling

117

eyes! Once the coveted portions had been duly distributed, all conversation ground to a salivating halt as we hesitated with bated breath before breaking our expectant forks into the first mouth-watering morsel.

A moment of complete, unadulterated silence hung poised in the air as we savoured the immorality of the sensuous sweetness. Finally, Melissa gasped, "Without a doubt, this is *the* very best dessert I have ever tasted in my entire life!" Then she shook her head, sighed and added, "I wish I could bake something like this, but I can't ... *because I'll eat it!*"

That comment sparked a lively discussion about weight and food and dieting in which six of the eight dinner guests revealed that they, too, avoided baking because the temptation to overeat was overpowering. As Shirley put it, "When I whip up a batch of Crowd Pleasin' Double Fudge Brownies for my kids, the pan suddenly seems to spring alive, beckoning relentlessly to my subconscious until my willpower completely dissolves and I succumb. And once that happens ...

*Once I start eating ... **I just can't seem to stop** until I've eaten the whole thing — or most of it!*"

PLEASE, SOMEBODY EAT THIS UP!

As Eleanor's dinner party was winding down, she asked if anyone cared for more of her Tipsy Rum and Eggnog Supreme Cheesecake. (Yes, it tasted as decadent as it sounds!) While people hummed and hawed over deciding what to do ... wanting to have another piece, but wondering if they could find the room or afford the calories, Eleanor made an interesting appeal to the potential dessert-takers, "Please!" she pleaded. "Somebody eat this up. If not, I'll polish off the rest of it the moment you all walk out the door!"

FOOD FOR THOUGHT

Why is it, that once we start eating something that tastes good, we just can't seem to stop until we've eaten the whole thing — or most of it!!

THE ALL-OR-NOTHING MENTALITY

I think one of the hardest habits for a chronic dieter to break is the ***all-or-nothing*** mentality. Its claws simply dig too tenaciously into our dieting psyche! You see, our overwhelming desire to be thinner creates this all-consuming need within us to diet; which in turn, nurtures an abnormal frame of mind towards food. And eventually, this unhealthy mind-set penetrates even further into our eating habits, becoming so ingrained that we unwittingly condition ourselves to starve when we are on a diet, and to overeat when we are not. Take myself and the pancakes, for example.

At that point in my life, there was absolutely no way I could have one or two pancakes. I had to totally abstain or go all the way — ***starve or binge***. A happy medium simply did not exist for me. And Rosemary was the same. She wanted to forego the Regent for tea, because once there she would feel compelled to overeat. Likewise, Eleanor cringed at the thought of having any dessert left over because she knew she would attack it once her guests had gone.

 FOOD FOR THOUGHT

In essence, fueled by a driving dissatisfaction with our bodies, we become so hooked on dieting in the pursuit of thinness, that our relationship with food becomes totally perverted. And as a result ... we find it impossible to eat in moderation like a normal human being!

119

THE NIGHT EATER

In addition to being a certifiable **all-or-nothing eater** (and to complicate my situation further), I was a documented **night eater** and **stand up eater.** Whether these two problems were outgrowths of the first, or independently born, I don't know. But I do know this. I would justifiably get up during the night to go to the bathroom. And then, in a drugged state of somnambulism, I'd make a direct beeline for the kitchen ... where I would stand, knife in hand, slivering away to the pacifying whir of the dishwasher!

Subsequently, upon awakening the next morning and returning to "the scene of the crime," I'd be horrified to witness the aftermath of my eating spree — crumbs all over the breadboard and half the cake "missing." Do you think I'd have breakfast? Not on your life! I wasn't hungry and felt too disgusted with myself. How about lunch? No way! But ... as the afternoon wore on and evening approached, my conviction waned as my hunger grew. And chances were, I didn't possess the mental or physical wherewithal to prevent myself from repeating the whole sick process again.

THE STAND UP EATER

Company's coming for dinner, and you have just finished preparing the grand finale — Sex In A Pan! To ensure it tastes as good as it looks, you decide to sample a thin sliver (after all, you haven't made this before; and besides, you've been too busy to have any lunch!). So, standing at the kitchen counter, you cut off a sliver. Then another (to even out the edge). And ... another (to even out the edge you just evened out!).

Finally, feeling more than satisfied that dessert is acceptable, you look down aghast! You can hardly believe your eyes! Staring back at you is a gaping hole almost one quarter the size of the pan. You've eaten almost one quarter of that Sex In A Pan by standing there slivering away at it! The "evidence" could not be more damning!

Now at this point in time, three things are for certain. One, you are *not* going to serve dessert at the table (if you did, everyone would wonder who had attacked it!). Two, you are *not* going to have a piece with your guests *like a normal human being*! And three, after the last person has left and you are cleaning up, you are *not* going to be able to keep your hands off that stupid Sex In A Pan. Oh no. Inevitably, you will once again find yourself standing at the kitchen counter slivering away at it!

 FOOD FOR THOUGHT

Whenever I ate like this, my conscience became immersed in the uneasy guilt of my actions. It was then I would berate myself and repeatedly lament, "Why can't I simply sit down at the dining room table and have a piece in a civilized manner with everyone else ... like a normal human being?"

Why?!

THE RESULTS ARE EQUALLY DISASTROUS!

It doesn't matter *where* you eat standing up (at the kitchen counter, directly out of the refrigerator, at a cocktail party — anywhere!), or *when* you eat at night (after supper, in the wee hours of the morning, or some time in-between). The results are equally disastrous! Because unless you have a concrete point of reference such as the sides of the aforementioned cake pan, you have no way of accurately gauging just how much food you have actually channeled into your mouth!

In addition, neither the *stand up eater* or *night eater* has the pleasure of fully tasting and properly enjoying what they are eating. Because the *stand up eater* is so busy trying to balance food on the tips of her fingers or the edge of a knife, and cram it into her mouth before it falls — that she tastes little or nothing at all. While the *night eater* is half-asleep, neither fully cognizant of what she is doing at the time, nor able to remember the next morning exactly what she ate, let alone how it tasted!

THE CAR EATER

Have you ever walked past a bakery and been pulled through the door by the tantalizing aromas? And once inside, have you been unable to resist purchasing a dozen fresh out of the oven Boston Creams/Apple Fritters/ or _____ (you fill in the treat) because they are your husband's/friend's/child's/ _____ favourite ... only to find yourself devouring several in the car on the way home? Thus, as you pull into the driveway with sticky fingers, crumb-filled lap, and a megaguilty conscience, have you ever felt compelled to eat several more donuts to even out the number? Because after all, who buys eight or nine donuts? That way you can pretend you only bought half a dozen to begin with, and save yourself the embarrassment of incriminating questions over the whereabouts of those missing!

 FOOD FOR THOUGHT

Honestly, wouldn't the donuts taste better and wouldn't you feel better if you waited until you arrived home before you ate?! If you made yourself a nice cup of tea or coffee, and then sat down and thoroughly savoured the taste of one donut along with your beverage?

Wouldn't this be far better mentally (you are in control and guilt-free) and physically (you are not subjecting your body to binge abuse)?

What a contrast to frantically shoving those stupid donuts into your mouth; attempting to eat and drive at the same time, hardly able to taste what you are furiously propelling into your mouth!

Speaking of which, have you ever observed how some people eat?

THE INHALER VS. THE NIBBLER

It was after work on a Friday night. As my thin co-worker Joan and I ordered Deluxe Cheese Hamburger Platters for dinner, we both commented upon how famished we were. Consequently, when our meals came, I proceeded to wolf mine down in record time fully expecting her to do the same. But I was wrong!

I found myself finished well ahead of Joan, only to be left sitting and watching in rapt, burping attention as she ate. Not only was I mesmerized by the placid pace of her eating (for someone who was supposed to be starving!), but also by the time she took to be so fastidious with her food. Joan was actually scrutinizing her french fries, **selecting the best ones to eat**! and leaving those unworthy of her discriminating standards to suffer unchosen on her plate.

 FOOD FOR THOUGHT

Has it occurred to you (as it repeatedly has to me) that fat and thin people have distinctly different eating styles?

I mean, don't slim people seem to eat in virtual slow motion; nibbling at their food in a somewhat loving manner as they take the time to savour the flavour? Meanwhile, at the other end of the table sit their heavier counterparts, shoveling in huge mouthfuls machine-gun style (appearing not to properly chew or taste any of it!).

A generalization? Yes, because I do know heavy people who eat slowly and thin ones who don't. However, for the most part, I find the opposite to be true ... which leads me to wonder why.

Is it because people with a weight problem guiltily inhale their food, knowing full well they shouldn't be eating it in the first place? Or are they greedily gobbling what lays before them in piggish anticipation of seconds? Or then again, are they overindulging today with the expectation of dieting tomorrow?

Whatever the reason, make a concerted effort to eat in an unhurried, dignified manner and in smaller bites. This will enable food to linger longer on your taste buds and maximize your enjoyment of it.

Furthermore, eating slowly naturally curbs the amount of food you eat (especially deadly seconds!). How so? Well, it takes fifteen to twenty minutes for your stomach to feel full after you have eaten. Therefore, eating slowly increases the likelihood you will feel fuller sooner and not be as tempted to reach for more!

THE CLOSET EATER

Do you know someone who is obese, who is always dieting, and who eats only a bite or two in front of you? Do you wonder how a person who supposedly exists on carrot and celery sticks became so heavy in the first place and remains that way? Well, it could be that the individual in question is a *closet eater*, someone who is just too ashamed of herself to eat among others. So, she picks and pokes and plays with food when she is in public, and overeats in private.

Janet is like that. She confesses to eating a full meal before going out for dinner because she hates people self-righteously examining her plate in search of something fattening.

And then there is Arlene, a two hundred and forty-three pound housewife and mother of two, whose husband Dennis is always on her case about her weight. Her response is to hide food in strategic places around the house — like the stash of mini Mars Bars she keeps in the linen closet; and the bag of Double Stuf Oreos underneath the laundry room sink. This hoarding tactic allows Arlene to eat without her spouse's knowledge, thereby avoiding his critical glare and deprecating comments.

THE NON-BREAKFAST EATER

Do you eat breakfast on a regular basis?

I doubt it.

How can I make that assumption? Because time and time again, when conversing with weight worriers, I have heard the same classic comment, "Well, I have nothing for breakfast ... except a cup of coffee."

Go ahead and ask someone who is heavy (or thinks they are), if they eat breakfast. In many cases, you'll find their reply one of disbelief and indignation. Not at your query, but at the fact *they don't eat breakfast,* and yet **they are still "fat!"** It's as if skipping breakfast should somehow absolve them of all past and present eating trespasses!

Before I developed a healthier relationship with food, I took great pride in not having breakfast. Now I see the futility of that practice but can also understand the method behind my madness. You see, I awoke almost every morning determined to continue my existing diet or resolved to begin a new one. In light of that, I irrationally thought I would get my dieting day off to a good start by "saving" my breakfast calories for later. Furthermore, I tried to eat as little as possible throughout the day for as long as I could bear. Thus, around the dinner hour — because I had been so "good" (and because I was absolutely famished!) — I would proceed to consume my quota of daily calories, *plus* the "saved" breakfast calories ten times over!

In retrospect, the irony now leaps right out at me. There I was, piously forsaking breakfast in order to stockpile its calories. How ridiculous! I mean, realistically, just how many calories exist in a small, nutritious breakfast? A boiled egg with a slice of toast and a glass of juice? ... A bowl of whole grain cereal topped with fresh fruit? Hardly any compared to those in a huge dinner devoured after a day of starvation. Or in a bag of chips demolished while watching TV at night. Or in the number inhaled during a raid of the kitchen in the wee hours of the morning.

However, when I was a chronic dieter, having no breakfast seemed like the right thing to do. At that point in my dieting life cycle, it made perfect sense. But now I know better. Now I know that people who skip breakfast only end up fatter at the end of the day!

THE BINGER/PURGER

Can you recall your last pig-out? At a Mexican restaurant, perhaps, where the Margaritas, Nachos, Enchiladas, and Chilies Rellenos never tasted better. And afterwards, were you so disgustingly stuffed you could hardly move? With extended, aching stomach, you swore never to let another refried bean or drop of tequila ever pass between your lips again! With extended, aching stomach, you vowed to join a weight loss group at the crack of dawn. With extended, aching stomach, you wished you could rid yourself of the agony after the ecstasy — by simply throwing up.

Jennifer does just that on a regular basis ... because, sadly, Jenny is bulimic. Her abnormal eating behaviour was triggered when she gained twenty pounds during her first year of living in a university dorm. As she puts it, "I want to eat and I want to be thin." So, she eats and eats and overengorges on her favourite foods, and then promptly puts her fingers down her throat and makes herself throw up. In between binges (when her conscience gets the better of her), Jenny diets.

Is that any way to eat?! To live?!

(Note: If you are like Jenny and suffer from bulimia, you should seek professional help.)

———————

**FINAL FOOD FOR THOUGHT ON
ABNORMAL EATING**

If you have a weight problem, or if you think you have a weight problem, or if you are continually dissatisfied with your body, chances are you have developed into an abnormal eater. And the ludicrous outcome of abnormal eating behaviour, regardless of how it is manifested (all-or-nothing; standing up, throwing up, et cetera; or combinations thereof) is this.

Abnormal eaters end up consuming far more food (and usually higher calorie food at that!) than if they just ate *normally*. Furthermore, abnormal eating promotes a barrage of negative metabolic consequences that often leaves people even heavier and unhappier.

Thus ... if you could just sit down and eat *normal* portions in a *normal* fashion like a *normal* person; the guilt would not creep in, and the hating yourself could not take over, and the purging of your eating sins would not be such a dominating force in your life. And above all, the whole vicious cycle would not continue!

That is why it is critical for you to take an honest look at your eating habits and determine whether or not you are a partial or full-fledged abnormal eater. Once you can identify and acknowledge this, you have made yet another strategic move towards normalizing your relationship with food. The next logical and important step is to try to figure out what causes you to overeat.

Chapter 10

Reasons for Overeating

As you read this chapter and digest its contents, I'd like you to bear the following in mind.

First, it is perfectly normal and natural to overeat — *occasionally*. Everyone does! However, when overeating occurs on a regular and patterned basis, it signals a problem.

Second, reasons for food abuse are rarely black and white, but rather shades of abnormal-eating gray; which often makes it difficult to clearly pinpoint the real source of the problem. Take worrying, for example. Many people turn to food when they are worried about "something" … a pending job layoff, a failing relationship, a wayward child. However, while their initial concern is over a specific situation; related reactions (such as depression, anger, frustration), plus other unrelated difficulties, may arise to cloud the original issue.

In addition, reasons for overeating can vacillate from day to day. Someone may have overeaten yesterday for one reason. Today for another. And tomorrow for an entirely different one. Perhaps all the while suppressing a major underlying anxiety and using their weight to shield themselves against it.

Therefore, after reading this chapter, if you still have trouble identifying the catalyst(s) of your abnormal eating; I suggest you keep a food diary for several weeks. In it, list the particulars of your eating habits — what you eat, how much, when and where, and *most importantly*, how you *feel* at the time. Because you may be overeating in response to something that is eating you! If so, you can move towards working through your problem(s) and eliminating your abnormal eating reaction to it.

But a word of caution. Do not expect your food diary to provide you with an instant cure. It is better to think of it as a beacon that can shed some light on your feelings and eating responses; and in doing so, illuminate the gateway leading towards a healthier relationship with food.

 FOOD FOR THOUGHT

Above all, remember that there are a multitude of reasons for overeating (including some not presented here). And these reasons are rarely cut and dried, but rather complex, interdependent, and deeply rooted!

STRESS/ WORRY/ BEING IN CONTROL

Are you stressed out? Tired and irritable? Sick of burning the candle at both ends only to find there are still not enough hours in the day? And as a result of this hectic merry-go-round lifestyle, are your eating habits and weight suffering? ... Then try this proven method (employed and enjoyed by millions!) to get you back on track and raring to go again!

Stress Diet

Breakfast

1/2 pink grapefruit
1 slice whole wheat toast (no butter, jam, or other toppings)
6 oz. skim milk (chilled)

Midmorning snack

the other half of the grapefruit
1 cup herbal tea (any flavour)

Lunch

4 oz. boiled chicken breast (no skin)
1 cup steamed lima beans (no butter or sauce)
1 Oreo Cookie

Midafternoon snack

3 Oreo Cookies
1 quart Rocky Road Ice Cream
1 jar Double Devil Fudge Sauce (heated in the microwave — if you can wait that long!)

Dinner

4 cans of lite beer
3 pieces of garlic bread
2 sides of onion rings
1 large Sausage, Pepperoni and Mushroom Pizza (double cheese)
1/2 a Sara Lee frozen Cheesecake (any variety) eaten directly from the freezer

Midevening snack

the rest of the package of Oreo Cookies
the other 1/2 of the Sara Lee Cheesecake

What an apt, comical description of how so many of us start off our dieting morning by eating cleanly and conscientiously, only to find ourselves going straight downhill as the day progresses and life's pressures mount along with our hunger! However, beneath the chuckles, there is truth in jest. Below the surface of this mock diet, hover some deep, pervasive insights. Let's take a closer look at the relationship between food and stress, followed by other reasons for abnormal eating.

FOOD WAS COMFORTING TO ME AT A TIME WHEN I NEEDED COMFORTING

Several years ago, Eleanor (a single, thirty-eight year old American State Department employee) was extremely depressed over her body. She said, "Pauline, I am beside myself. I am fifteen pounds **heavier** than my previous *top* weight! It's so bad, even my fat clothes are bursting at the seams! What am I going to do?!"

As we sat and discussed how and why she had ballooned up, Eleanor knew exactly what had happened. She confided that during the previous year, she fell into the bad habit of coming home after work to her cold, lonely apartment and stuffing herself with food. Then, somewhere between the hours of two and four in the morning, she would awaken and repeat the whole sick process again!

Eleanor admitted to being stressed out during that time; and attributed her unhealthy eating behavior to her frazzled mental state. A long term relationship had recently ended (and the fella who wouldn't marry her promptly tied the knot with someone he'd just met!). Her mother's health was deteriorating from Parkinson's disease. And Eleanor was extremely unhappy with a recent career move to the Washington, D.C. area. "So," she stated, "I simply turned to food because it was comforting to me at a time when I needed comforting. Food helped to alleviate the stress in my life."

But she wasn't so comforted a year later, when the emotional baggage she had been carrying around in her head was firmly implanted around her hips!

I PROMPTLY PARKED MYSELF BY THE BUFFET TABLE AND PROCEEDED TO SHOVEL ALL OF THE MOST FATTENING FINGER FOOD INTO MY MOUTH

And then there was the time I overdosed on Coconut Cream Cheese Icing. We were having company for dinner, and the frosting was intended to adorn our dessert (a scrumptious Carrot Cake), not my derriere! However that morning, I stood at the kitchen counter "testing" just a little of the frosting. Then a little more. And a little more. Until I eventually found myself spooning gobfuls of it into my gaping mouth. Afterwards, I lay sprawled on the living room floor ... physically ill from the icky sweetness I had ingested, and emotionally heartsick over my abnormal eating. "Why?!" I kept repeating over and over again. "Why do I behave this way with food when it only makes me hate myself even more?!"

Now the situation that prompted my demise was nothing major or earth-shattering. In fact, you may find it so trivial, as to border on the ridiculous. But innocuous as the circumstances were, I was extremely distraught over them.

It was December, and as the seventh grade class advisor, I had the "privilege" of overseeing the Junior High Christmas Dance. But my charges were highly distracted and disorganized because the event fell the weekend before their very first set of semester exams. Thus, they couldn't get their act together when it came the specifics of the dance such as decorating the gymnasium.

As for me, I, too, felt uptight and preoccupied. While the students were studying for their exams, I was busy preparing mine. In addition, I had to mark those tests, calculate my semester grades, and fill out report cards — all before Christmas break. Consequently, I allowed myself to become overstressed, overtired, and overly perturbed at not being in control of everything. Which unfortunately, led to this.

In the midst of everything, I went on an eating bender at a tree-trimming party. I promptly parked myself in front of a buffet table and shoveled all of the most fattening finger food I could lay my hands on into my mouth as fast as I could! But ... the situation gets even worse, if you can believe it!

I arrived home from the tree-trimming party that night feeling like a stuck pig; and cursing myself for having no willpower.

Now, in addition to the dance and exams and report cards, I was left carrying the extra weight (and guilt) of my untimely binge. *Just something more to worry about*! As I fell asleep that night, bloated and unhappy, my mind renewed its steady stream of angst, prompting me to vehemently vow to starve myself *forever*! if that's what it took to lose weight.

But, what was the first thing I did when I awoke the next morning? (I feel so embarrassed, I am almost too ashamed to tell you!) It was then I stood in the kitchen and ate spoonful after spoonful of that stupid Coconut Cream Cheese Icing?! A pig-out on top of a pig-out. *A double pig-out*!! Oh, God, *why*?!

 FOOD FOR THOUGHT

Isn't it strange how we turn to food in response to stress?

And what is even stranger and extremely ironic is that *eating doesn't solve our problem(s)!*

On the contrary, eating only serves to compound the situation by making us doubly unhappy. Because added to our initial worry, is the worry created by our overeating.

Thus, the by-product of overeating in response to worry, is more worry followed by more overeating! (Are you with me so far?... Stick with it!)

And if you think that sounds complicated, consider what transpires if the original source of your worry (and reason for overeating) is your bodily dissatisfaction. Take Kristie, for example.

Kristie says, "I try to live with my weight, but it's hard for me to be happy when I'm so unhappy with my body. And when I am unhappy, I eat. This in turn makes me even unhappier, which makes me eat even more and become even unhappier!" (Talk about a vicious cycle!)

133

FOOD FOR THOUGHT

Are you beginning to see how complex and inter-related the reasons for abnormal eating really are? And we've only begun to scratch the surface!

TRANSFERENCE

Have you ever had to do something you did *not* want to do; or had a terrible fight with someone ... only to find yourself stuffing your face with food?

In retrospect, I think I overate at times to transfer the source of my concern from what was bothering me to my weight — and more specifically, to those parts of my body I despised so much, my big hips and bum! For example, as an English teacher, whenever I had a stack of essays to evaluate (an ominous task because of the subjectivity involved), I found myself inevitably heading to the kitchen and pigging out. Then, rather than being upset at having to grade, I became upset at myself for having overeaten. In reality, I directed my anxiety inward, away from the external source.

And the irrational aspect of this transference, was that I still had to mark those papers (the initial perpetrator of my anxiety) whether I overate or not!

HAPPINESS

Another possible reason for overeating is difficult to put into words (and might sound totally bizarre to those who haven't experienced it!). It has to do with ultimate happiness. You see, I have been blessed with a terrific childhood and wonderful life up to now (succeeding in just about whatever I endeavoured, except, of course, to be pencil thin). And because I am so fortunate, I wonder if I overate to give myself something to worry about. Crazy as it may sound, perhaps I needed to fret over my weight ... because if I didn't, there would be a void in my life; nothing to be constantly striving towards.

PERFECTIONISM

And then there is this to consider. Was I such a little perfectionist, that I couldn't stand the thought of not having the picture perfect body? I had a perfectly lovely, perfectly functioning body — but it wasn't perfect enough for me!

SCAPEGOATING

Allison uses her body as an excuse for her failures. She blames her weight for her inability to find Mr. Right and keep him (Geoffrey had left her and married another woman). To advance in her career (prettier, thinner girls were by-passing her with promotions). And to be a happier person (how can she be happy when she is so fat and ugly?). Allison repeatedly laments, "If only I weren't so fat, then I would be able to _____ ."

ANGER/FRUSTRATION

"I simply can't stand my new boss!" Jessica stated emphatically as we drove to aerobics. "I mean, I really try hard to get along with him, and not let him get to me. But, it's impossible. *He's* impossible!"

"What's the problem?" I inquired concerned.

"Well, for starters," Jessica replied with a big sigh, "he's demanding, critical, intimidating, and unappreciative. And to add insult to injury, he thoroughly embarrassed me in front of some co-workers this afternoon. He makes me so angry! Do you know what I just finished doing? ... I'm ashamed to admit this, but as soon as I walked through the door after work, I headed straight to the kitchen and went on a massive food bender. And now I am sooo angry with myself! That man *is driving me to eat!*"

FOOD FOR THOUGHT

Again, food seems to provide instant consolation during troubled times, doesn't it?

I mean, if you are angry/ depressed/ _____ (you fill in the frame of mind), isn't there a strange, almost perverse sense of satisfaction in grabbing handful after handful of M & M's, for example, and throwing those comforting capsules into your mouth; crunching down and feeling them crackle apart ... and then reveling in their sensual smoothness as they squish in and around your taste buds. And can't you just feel your anger/depression/ _____ slowly soften and dissipate along with the melting chocolate?

As Ellen confided, "Some people turn to alcohol or drugs, but I turn to food. Whenever I'm upset, I simply sink my teeth into something fattening and eat my troubles away. It makes me feel so good — *immediately*!"

BOREDOM

Ginny is bored to tears! She doesn't work outside the home, and has no children and few interests. Consequently, in the mid-to-late afternoon (much to her dismay!), she finds herself heading towards the kitchen accompanied by a formidable companion — her uncontrollable urge to eat. She ashamedly confessed to me one morning that she had baked a batch of Fudge Ecstasies the day before and devoured *the entire pan*! before her husband arrived home from his business trip that night!

TASTE

In the midst of writing this book, I overate one evening at a dinner party. This so rarely happens since I have come to terms with my body and food, that I was eager to analyze why. I came up with the following possibilities:

1) I was tired and it was hot (98 degrees and 90% humidity in Bangkok).

2) I was eight months pregnant, and I felt I should eat a little more for the baby.

3) I was feeling out of sorts that night due to a first-time bout of hemorrhoids. (Not only were they painful and bothersome, but they also ended up being one more unpleasant aspect of pregnancy that my mother hadn't warned me about!)

4) The meal was absolutely mouth-watering!

These were all of the probable reasons. But one in particular stood out ... the exquisite taste of the food. Lightly battered tempura of fresh shrimp, baby corn, cauliflowerettes, green beans, onions, and a succulent white fish. Everything was so irrepressibly delicious, I continued to eat and eat and eat. Thoroughly relishing the repast, until I began to feel unbearably uncomfortable.

 FOOD FOR THOUGHT

Now, why did I stretch my stomach past the point of enjoyment into the sphere of indigestion? I mean, does eating twice as much of something make it taste twice as good?

For that matter ...

Does putting twice as much into your mouth at one time double its pleasure?

Of course not!

137

Just think about it … Aren't the first mouthfuls of any food really the tastiest? I mean, don't you find those initial bites of that Coconut Cream Pie, or Fettuccine Alfredo, or Grand Marnier Cheesecake really the most delicious? And, isn't it much more emotionally and physically satisfying to take the time to slowly savour each and every forkful of your first and only regular-sized helping?

Keep that in mind, the next time you find yourself salivating over seconds before you've paid proper lip service to firsts!

THE ENERGIZER

At times, I know I overate out of sheer exhaustion as a by-product of my overachiever personality. You see, I would push myself all day long to accomplish twice as much as possible. And to top everything off, I added to my overburdened stress load by dieting and exercising like a woman possessed. Consequently, I'd arrive home at night starving and exhausted. And then, because I still had so many things I wanted to do, I would eat to physically and emotionally give myself the energy to continue. In essence, I'd run myself ragged and use food as an energizer to keep me going!

THE TRANQUILLIZER

Now, what may sound totally incomprehensible is that the complete opposite was also true. Sometimes when I did manage to get through a hectic day in control (accomplishing a great deal *and* dieting and exercising perfectly), I'd find myself so over-tired and overhungry that I'd have difficulty falling asleep at night. During those times, food acted as a sedative (not an ener-gizer) that enabled me to put my complaining stomach and over-worked mind and body to rest.

Furthermore, I now realize that one of the reasons I couldn't sleep was that I was wired on caffeine! As a substitute for food,

I was drinking potfuls of tea throughout the day, which inevitably led to a severe case of caffeine overload and its associated insomnia!

THE MEDICATOR

Carol confided, "I've gained 15 pounds and I know why. I am currently in the process of divorcing my second husband (who is an alcoholic) and I am using food to medicate my emotions. I realize this is a band-aid approach, but food makes me feel better right now."

THE SHIELD

Carol went on to say, "In fact, I don't really mind carrying the extra weight. I think it repels men and keeps them from bothering me. At this point in my life, I don't want to be involved with anyone. I just want to be left alone."

 FOOD FOR THOUGHT

Carol's reasons for overeating demonstrate just how multifaceted and complicated a person's relationship with food can be. Because Carol is not overweight for one reason, but several intertwined!

THE SABOTEUR

One January, in the midst of my first postholiday diet of the new year, Darlene invited me to dinner in celebration of her boyfriend's birthday. I declined, fully explaining my dieting situation. But Darlene wouldn't take "no" for an answer and insisted I attend. I finally acquiesced, but later wished I hadn't! Everything was fine until dessert when I said, "Thanks, but no thanks." to her Incredibly Sinful Kahlua 'n Cream Marshmallow

Fudge Mousse. In response, Darlene flew into a rage, and laced into a five minute tirade about my ill manners. I sat there in stunned disbelief and horror!

I was mortified at being embarrassed in front of my dinner companions!, but ... I was equally mortified at Darlene's behaviour. I was a guest in her home (a guest who didn't want dessert!), and I was being treated like a common criminal (and a rude one at that)! Even more infuriating and unbelievably ironic is that Darlene, herself, is a chronic dieter. In fact, just the November before, she had dogmatically stuck to a month-long liquid diet! I wonder how she would have felt then if I had badgered her to eat, and showered insults upon her when she declined?

And above all, *she was supposed to be my friend*!

FOOD FOR THOUGHT

Why are there so many persistent expectations and demands surrounding food?

I mean, why was Darlene so unreasonable over my refusal of her dessert? And what makes others guilty of similar behaviour?

Are these people so insecure that everyone has to "ooh" and "aah" over their culinary expertise? Or do they equate rejection of their food with rejection of themselves? Or are they jealous when they see others dieting, when they think/ wish/ know they should? If so, does this make them want to sabotage the efforts of well-intentioned weight watchers by pushing unwanted food and comments upon them ...

"I baked this especially for you — I know it's your favourite!"

"Go ahead. Have seconds! You can start dieting again tomorrow."

"Come on! Keep me company … One eensy-weensy little piece isn't going to hurt." (*Oh yeah!*)

HUNGER

Have you ever dieted religiously for a period of time, only to find yourself suddenly going berserk with food?! Propelled by a raging appetite, you insanely undo all of your painstaking efforts by virtually raping the kitchen of anything edible!

 FOOD FOR THOUGHT

In the midst of one of these eating sprees, have you ever stopped to consider that you might be overeating because you are certifiably overhungry?

 FURTHER FOOD FOR THOUGHT

We need to listen more closely to what our bodies are saying, don't we?

Keep that in mind as you digest this.

BODY TALK

About once a month, Nancy embarks upon a chocolate binge. Her last one went like this. It was Friday afternoon and the end of a very hectic work week. Nancy was admittedly tired and hungry. On her way home, she stopped at a convenience store to buy a quart of milk, and impulsively purchased a package of chocolate chips to make some cookies. Unfortunately, however, upon returning to her car, she ripped the bag apart; and amidst a flurry of flying chipits drove home!

And what do you think Nancy proceeded to do the moment she entered her apartment?

Possessed by the invisible force of a demonic craving unsatiated by the bag of chipits, she furiously rummaged through the kitchen in search of something else "chocolatey." Finding nothing but a packaged brownie mix, she whipped up a batch in a frenzy, eating half of the ready-made chocolate frosting as she impatiently waited for the brownies to bake.

Once those brownies emerged from the oven, Nancy tried desperately to apply the icing; but to no avail — the hot surface reduced the frosting to slippery rivulets of drooling goop! Not to be deterred, Nancy then sat at the kitchen table with a wedge of hot brownie in one hand and a spoonful of icing in the other, alternating mouthfuls.

Having burnt her tongue on the brownies, she remembered the half-eaten carton of Chocolate Ripple Ice Cream in the freezer and proceeded to polish that off. Two hours after her chocolate binge began, Nancy lay on the couch in bloated, burping guilt and remorse. She was so engorged she could hardly move, and so full of contempt for herself she just wanted to curl up and die. The next morning, Nancy started her period.

 FOOD FOR THOUGHT

Why do we pig out like this!?

Is it the taste of the food? Or the physical pleasure of the act ... the crunching down and breaking into something hard; the melting dissipation of creamy softness upon the taste buds? Or, is it the chemical effect of the food upon the body?

Let's examine this last possibility a little further. The notorious pickle-and-ice-cream-type cravings of pregnant women being a classic case in point.

LIVER PÂTÉ AND PEACHES

When I was pregnant, I *had* to have my Egg McMuffin and grapefruit juice every morning (much to my husband's chagrin!). I craved Spinach Salads any time of the day or night. Oatmeal Chocolate Chip Cookies during the seventh month. Liver pâté the eighth month. And tinned peaches with cottage cheese the last week. When Andrea was expecting, she had an insatiable appetite for Banana Splits; whereas Melanie coveted any and all Greek food. What precipitates these definitive food preferences in pregnant women?

Well, I believe that when a person is driven by an intense burning desire to eat a certain "something" (whether female or male; pregnant or not!), their body is trying to communicate what it wants and needs in the only way it knows how. Furthermore, research confirms that cravings can extend beyond the bounds of the purely physical (i.e. your body needs salt, so you crave it) and into the realm of our emotions and how certain foods make us feel. Take chocolate, for instance, which is known to elicit feelings of well-being. And then take Nicole, who turns to Old-Fashioned Fudge Cake (the kind she ate as a child in the warmth and security of her grandmother's kitchen) whenever she feels down. (Ah, good old "comfort" food! We all have ours, don't we?)

So what does this mean?

It means that there is a physiological connection between how we feel and what we eat. Hence, cravings and binges are not always a reflection of poor willpower!

However, we must not treat this as a licence to eat. We must not overjustify our overeating with a string of lame excuses … "I'm starting my period soon." "I'm pregnant and fat anyway, so what's a few more pounds?" "Well, my body must need this, so what the heck!"

On the contrary, I propose we listen thoughtfully to our bodies and deal sensibly with what they have to say. Once we can

143

accurately identify a bodily craving and then emotionally deal with it in a rational manner, we have made another important step towards normalizing our relationship with food.

Take Nancy, for example. When she is driven wild by her premenstrual desire to rape chocolate once a month, she should take the time to acknowledge the source and handle it more effectively. Nancy could:

1) Go to a public place like the Dairy Queen.

2) Order a Hot Fudge Brownie Delight (with chocolate chipits or a reasonable facsimile sprinkled on top if she so desires).

3) Sit down in that public setting.

4) **Drink two glasses of water before eating** (more about that to come in the last chapter!).

And then,

5) Enjoy that chocolatey, ice creamy treat in a CIVILIZED manner!

By reacting to an "attack" in this way, Nancy would be eating some chipits (not an entire bag). Two brownies (instead of a whole panful). Six ounces of ice milk (not half a carton of ice cream). And a portion of chocolate syrup (rather than a full tin of frosting)!

 FOOD FOR THOUGHT

Now, wouldn't this make more sense and be less self-destructive? ... As well as less fattening?

Besides, *if you do not satiate extremely powerful cravings with a controlled response*, you are only setting yourself up for bigger trouble! Because unsatiated cravings will persist and lead to destructive, full-blown binges if left unheeded (regardless of how many carrot and celery sticks you try to placate yourself with!). Believe me, it is better to give your body what it demands — within reason! — and be fully satisfied.

I truly believe that as weight watchers and worriers, if we paid as much attention to what our bodies are saying, as we do to the intricate requirements of certain diets ... we would save ourselves much of the physical and mental anguish of perpetual dieting!

AN EATER FOR ALL REASONS

Ashley overeats on and off and she knows it. When trying to analyze "why" over lunch one day, she said something that succinctly sums up the feelings of many of us. In all earnestness, Ashley said, "Pauline, I've kept a food diary as you've suggested. I've also given a lot of thought to my feelings and eating habits. And, I've come to this conclusion.

I don't overeat for just one particular reason. *I eat for all of them*! I eat when I am happy, when I am sad; if I am bored, depressed, stressed out. You name it, and I'll eat because of it. I *love* food and I *love* eating! But ... at the same time, I *hate* the way my body looks!"

What is someone like Ashley to do? What should you do? What can anyone do to normalize relations between themselves and food?

Throughout this book, we have examined many facets of The Dieting Game. It's time now for you to become a winner! It's time to take a realistic look at solutions to your problem — and of those, the most viable, healthy and successful solution of all!

Chapter 11

Solutions

After worrying incessantly about my bum and hips for the majority of my life. And after dieting repetitively and unsuccessfully to get rid of them. And after continually exercising in vain to attain the svelte-like figure I desperately desired, I have finally come to terms with myself and my body.

For the first time since I can remember, I am able to behave like a truly normal person when it comes to food. My every waking moment is not consumed with thinking and worrying about it. I can eat salads with dressing now. I have sour cream on my baked potatoes. I do not dread buffet tables. I do not hate socializing. I can actually make a dessert and sit down and enjoy it with guests, instead of heading robotically towards the refrigerator the moment the company is out the door!

Today, I am able to eat what I want, enjoy it, and not feel guilty afterwards. If what I am having doesn't taste good, I don't eat it. If I am feeling full, I don't finish it. If I eat something fattening, I don't feel compelled to rush out and burn it off through exercise.

I am no longer a prisoner of food! *I am the one in control now!* Given my former eating habits, this is a stupendous accomplishment for me!

And it is such a fantastic feeling!! Gone are the constant minutes, hours, days, weeks, and years of endless worry over what I am eating, what I have eaten, and what I wished I could eat. The albatross has slipped from my neck, and I am no longer burdened with the emotional baggage of perpetually thinking about food and yearning to be thinner.

I have succeeded!

But how can you do the same? How can you come to terms with your body and food for the rest of your life?

Whether you are a little or a lot overweight. Whether you *"think"* you are fat. Or whether you are trying to reshape or reduce a certain body part, it is time to exorcise (no, *not* exercise!) yourself from the fat trap!

Here's how.

STEP ONE — THE "SOLE"-UTION

To begin with, you have to realize that the solution to your problem lies solely within you ("sole"-ution). Friends may help. Weight watching groups and companies may counsel. Spouses may provide incentives. But, your mentors and supporters *can not* be by your side twenty-four hours a day to keep you on the dieting straight and narrow.

I mean, realistically, will your best friend be able to rush to your rescue at two in the morning, after you've had an enormous fight with a loved one and are eating your "weigh" through the kitchen? Will your diet clinic be open on Christmas Day when you are experiencing a panic attack about keeping holiday goodies like Rum and Eggnog, and Shortbread Cookies at bay (not to mention the turkey dinner resplendent with all the trimmings!)?

In the final analysis, as unsettling as it may be, the ultimate responsibility lies with and within *you* — *alone*! Which brings us to the next step.

STEP TWO — THE "SOUL"-UTION

At this point, you need to find a quiet place where you will be undisturbed for a good half hour. (If you are a woman with children, this will most likely be some time past midnight! Once we've met everyone else's needs, we feel free to attend to our own — but, that's another topic and another book!) Now, close your eyes and take a few deep relaxing breaths to clear your mind.

Next, probe reflectively into the inner recesses of your psyche and have an objective heart-to-heart talk with yourself (the "soul"-ution). And during this private conversation, I want you to honestly evaluate how you feel about your body and your relationship with food. Your analysis might include comments such as ...

"I am ashamed/ hate/ dislike/ _____ my pot belly/ saddlebag hips/ midriff bulge/ _____."

"I am sick and tired of worrying about food all the time."

"I have tried just about every diet going and I am still fat and unhappy."

"What can I do?"

"What am I prepared to do?"

Now hold onto your thoughts! Because before I outline the available options, I'd like you to contemplate the *soul*-searching revelations of Cindy. Remember her?

Cindy was the school teacher who faithfully stuck to her eating regime (reinforced with diet pills) for seven tedious, frustrating months of slow weight loss — only to immediately balloon up again over the summer. Consequently, when I first saw Cindy after the holidays, I was shocked at how fat she had quickly become. Furthermore, I was hesitant to ask what had happened lest it further heighten her disappointment and humiliation. But surprisingly enough, Cindy was very willing to share her thoughts with me. So amidst chattering students, in a jiggling school bus returning from a field trip, Cindy talked while I sat mesmerized.

What transpired was a fascinating, suspended moment in time for me!

As Cindy spoke, I felt a tidal wave of heightened awareness and assuredness empower me. Her words struck a resonant déjà vu chord that reverberated deep within my sole and rattled the chains of dieting demons I thought I had put to rest forever. Only a short time before, I was making exactly the same statements in exactly the same mystified manner. I could identify *what* was happening in relation to myself and my weight, but not *why*. Like Cindy, I was at a loss to help myself even though the answer lay clearly before me!

As I sat listening, it dawned on me that Cindy was succinctly echoing the thoughts, feelings, and frustrations harboured by weight watchers and worriers the world over. However, this time, I was in the privileged position of being on the outside looking in. As a result, I was mentally able to respond to each of her comments with amazing clarity and confidence. I had been that route before and was no longer "lost!" I had reached my destination, and listened in rapt attention as she struggled to find hers.

REFLECTIONS ON DIETING

While no two weight problems are exactly the same, you will be surprised at the number of common dieting denominators Cindy unknowingly identified during our conversation on that bus. And what proved utterly mind-boggling was this.

Cindy's analysis of her dieting holds the key that will unlock the door of her self-imprisonment. Her past experiences clearly contain the answer to her weight problem (and yours!). See if you can glimpse the illuminating light at the end of Cindy's dieting tunnel.

Here is what Cindy said, and here is what I thought.

POINT 👈👉 COUNTERPOINT #1

Cindy: *"Whenever I lose weight, I regain it once I stop dieting."*

Myself: Aha!! The Yo-Yo Syndrome.

Repetitive dieting actually undermines our honest attempts to lose weight by forcing our bodies to become more energy efficient and function at a slower metabolic rate ... until they perceive that *the famine (and any threat thereof) is truly over*! Furthermore, our famine sensitive systems simultaneously grasp every opportunity to reclaim and stockpile as much weight as possible in anticipation of further deprivation. Thus (much to our frustration and chagrin!), when we stop dieting and start eating more than our bodies have been conditioned to receiving, we gain unsubstantiated weight.

POINT 👈👉 COUNTERPOINT #2

Cindy: *"I lost all that weight and now I am bigger than ever."*

Myself: Not only do people gain weight after dieting, but they also tend to gain in leapfrog fashion ... often hopping past their previous *top weight* to reset newer, heavier ones. Why? Because a frequently dieted body ultimately attempts to reattain its prediet poundage — and then some! — as added protection against the next onslaught of starvation.

POINT 👈👉 COUNTERPOINT #3

Cindy: *"There seems to be a fine line for my body between losing and gaining weight."*

Myself: Chronic dieting throws the body into a confused

state of metabolic flux. In essence, a metabolism doesn't know what to expect, feast or famine! And it is this uncertainty and instability that precludes the establishment of a stable *set weight*.

POINT 🖐️🖐️ *COUNTERPOINT #4*

Cindy: *"I try to live with my weight, but it's hard to be happy when I don't like my body. So I diet, but then I'm unhappy because dieting makes my life miserable!"*

Myself: One-half of a dieter's emotional plate is laden with dieting and the frustration of food deprivation. While the other half is burdened with the frustration of not dieting and the deprivation of the opportunity to be thinner. This leads to an endless circle of DIETING, WORRYING, NOT DIETING, WORRYING, DIETING, CHEATING, MORE WORRYING … And round and round it goes. Any way you look at it, dieters are caught in a no win situation hopelessly riddled with stress and unhappiness!

POINT 🖐️🖐️ *COUNTERPOINT #5*

Cindy: *"Each Monday I say to myself, 'I am going to start my diet today, and this time it's going to work for good!'"*

Myself: How many times have you made the same promise to yourself?

Isn't it demoralizing, humiliating and frustrating to fail *over* and *over* and *over* again … only to wake up to yet **another** Monday morning of "All the eggs, tomatoes and grapefruit you "desire!?" (Yuk!)

 FOOD FOR THOUGHT

Why haven't any of those Monday morning diets ever been permanently successful for you?

POINT ⟋⟍ COUNTERPOINT #6

Cindy: *"When I went to a diet doctor, I had to weigh-in on Mondays. Being weighed in front of a stranger kept me 'honest,' especially over the weekends."*

Myself: Outside support (whatever form it takes) helps. However, in the final analysis, the ultimate responsibility and decision making lies within *you*! Someone else will not always be there to weigh you. Someone else will not always be there to keep you "honest." That someone has to be *you* — alone!

POINT ⟋⟍ COUNTERPOINT #7

Cindy: *"I wish I could fall asleep and wake up in a month 15 pounds thinner."*

Myself: Dream on, Cindy! ... Because the reality of the situation is this.

Be it births, deaths, marriages, holidays (*regardless* of the time, place or occasion) one thing's for sure — a formidable army of edibles lies ready and waiting to attack your honourable intentions, making dieting downright intolerable and predictably disastrous!

(And besides, even if you could lose weight by isolating yourself from society, just how would you be able to maintain that weight loss once you reentered the real world and had to cope with all of that food again?)

POINT ⟋⟍ COUNTERPOINT #8

Cindy: *"Dieting puts a damper on a person's social life. I really enjoy people; but it's hard to entertain or attend social functions when I always have to worry about what I'm eating."*

Myself: It's not easy saying 'no' to food and it's not easy being unsociable. Either way we are emotionally and socially imprisoned by the restrictions of dieting, which circumscribe our capacity to truly enjoy our lives.

POINT ☞⟍⟍☞ COUNTERPOINT #9

Cindy: *"Exercise doesn't seem to make much of a difference."*

Myself: Exercise is **not** going to make a difference if your motives for doing so are misguided and unrealistic. If you expect, for example, to look like Jane Fonda after purchasing one of her videos and enthusiastically performing the exercises therein, you will be sorely disappointed. Why? Because exceptionally few people are born with a body like that. And exceptionally few people are capable of exercising their way into it!

Furthermore, the benefits of exercise are cumulative. Thus, an exercise program (no matter how intense) will end up doing precious little for you unless it is carried out on a **regular, moderate** basis over a period of time. Nor will it burn off as many calories as you feel you deserve in the process, or compensate for your overeating "sins!"

PUSHUPS FOR THE MIND!

*In the long run, you need to let go of the self-imposed roadblocks that prevent you from having a healthy relationship with exercise. Instead, you need to adopt the philosophy that ... regardless of your size and shape, **you are going to exercise regularly and moderately for the health of it!***

Believe me, you will save yourself a lifetime of the frustration and unhappiness that accompanies unmet, unrealistic expectations ... in exchange for the priceless physical and emotional rewards of a sensible exercise program *(that's 20 minutes, three times a week minimum!)*.

Cindy: *"I have to change my eating habits —forever."*

Myself: BINGO, Cindy!!! You've put your finger on the very heart of the matter.

Because no matter how many diets are attempted, *none* are going to be *permanently* successful unless followed in some "weigh," shape or form for the rest of your life!

Keep that in mind as you contemplate what lies ahead!

THE CROSSROADS

You are now standing at the threshold of one of the most critical stages leading to your dieting metamorphosis!

You are at the crossroads where *you* can make *the* crucial decision that will change your life forever!

But, this was one of the most difficult decisions I have made in my entire life. And I am a very logical, intelligent person who by all rights should never have been sucked into the quicksand of dieting in the first place!

Therefore, don't worry if you are unable to choose the right path right now. I'm not. Because I know how much courage you have demonstrated by journeying this far. And I also know that if it is too hard for you to move forward at this point in time, you will eventually return to this juncture armed with the ability and conviction to do so.

How can I be so sure?

Because the journey towards self-actualization involves a *process* — a process of self-discovery and acceptance that does *not* happen overnight! Believe me, I should know! It took an incredible amount of time, energy and diets (not to mention physical and emotional suffering!) before I could pull myself away from the suction of my dieting quagmire to realistically face the truth.

154

And when I finally did, I was able to look objectively at the possibilities that lay before me, and with crystal clear vision saw the following options.

Please weigh each with an open heart and mind.

YOUR FOUR OPTIONS

 **OPTION #1**

> **Continue to diet and/or overexercise ... intermittently in response to your weight loss and gain, or constantly as a means of trying to remain as thin as possible.**

When considering this option, you have to ask yourself ...

"In an attempt to possess the body I covet, am I prepared to live a life of perpetual denial, restricting myself to 950/ 850/ 750/ _____ calories a day ... measuring, weighing and worrying all the while?"

If your answer is yes, you must dedicate your entire existence to cohabiting with dieting (in some form or another) *for as long as you live*!

I CAN NOT STRESS THIS POINT ENOUGH!

If you choose to diet, you have to be prepared to stick with that diet for more than two weeks, two months, or two years. *You have to be prepared to stick with it for life*!

Option #1 — FOOD FOR THOUGHT

Personally, as you well know by now, I was thoroughly sick and tired of diets and dieting. In addition, I was frightened at the prospect of continuing to weight watch for the rest of my life when twenty years of doing so had failed to result in permanent success!

Now perhaps at this point in time you are still willing to diet. Perhaps you want to believe (as I did for so many years) that at least when you are dieting, you are "doing something" about your body. And that's your prerogative! But before you opt for that, sit down and ask yourself this.

If dieting works, then why aren't you thin and happy right now?

 OPTION #2

Have your fat surgically removed.

This time, you have to question …

"Am I willing to have surgery?" If so, "Am I able to afford it?"

And, "How will I feel, and what will I do if it is *not* successful?"

On the other hand, "How will I maintain my thin self if it is?"

 Option #2 — FOOD FOR THOUGHT

I was twenty-four hours away from liposuction! Scheduled for the operation November 23, 1985, I cancelled the day before. While I desperately desired those thinner hips, I simply could not justify subjecting my body to surgery for such a superficial reason.

156

And to be perfectly truthful, I was petrified that the operation would be a failure and I would be left with lumpy thighs or an lopsided bum. Or (horror upon horrors!), that I would regain the weight ... which actually happened to my friend, Cheryl! After liposuction, her thighs ballooned out to become heavier than they were to begin with. I guess that's what can happen when the side effect, and not the actual problem, is treated.

 OPTION #3

Eat whatever you want, when you want, and in the amounts you want.

With this option you say to yourself ...

"To hell with it! I'm fat whether I diet or not, so why bother?"

 Option #3 — FOOD FOR THOUGHT

While I was frustrated and exhausted with dieting, I simply could not see letting myself go completely and becoming any heavier. I had enough trouble liking myself the "weigh" I was. I knew for sure I would absolutely detest my body if I were any bigger!

 OPTION #4

If you want to feel better about yourself, your body, and your eating habits on a permanent basis, I can not urge you strongly enough to choose the following option! It will enable you to lead a happier and healthier life!!

How can I be so sure?

Because it worked for me when nothing else would!

How? Why! ...

Read on!

THE ULTIMATE SOLUTION

Ultimately, in order to be the very best you can possibly be physically and emotionally you have to normalize relations between your mind and body. A marriage of the two must take place within you. Therefore, in a moment of calm, honest introspection, you have to step back and take everything into consideration (your metabolism, body type, body image, society, diets, dieting, exercising, abnormal eating, and reasons for abnormal eating) and realistically assess who you are and where you are at bodywise.

Now this may be unsettling! For you might not like what you see. But however difficult, you must force yourself to do this!

The next step is to identify those parts of your body you can change; and *accept those you can not*! For example, you *can* do something about your hair (with minimal effort). You *can* do something to improve your muscle tone (this involves a dedicated commitment). And, you *can* do something about your abnormal eating habits (this will be a major undertaking). But as emphasized throughout this book, you have to *accept* that you can do **very little** or **nothing at all**! about certain aspects of your body.

And it is this self-acceptance that symbolizes the pivotal turning point in normalizing relations between your mind and body. For example, my dietitis was well on the road to recovery when I reached this understanding of myself.

"I, PAULINE, have a bigger bum in relation to the rest of my body. *But*, that is the way I was born, and I am going to *accept* this and like myself for who I am. Because I have attempted everything (short of surgery) to physically alter my shape. And in the whole scheme of things, it is ridiculous to be so caught up in the size of my bum when I have the love of family and friends, and an unhandicapped body, and everything else to be so physically and emotionally thankful for!"

And you have to embrace a similar mind-set! You must accept yourself for who you are bodywise *at this very moment in time* (imperfections and all).

For example …

"Today, I am 153/ 177/ _____ pounds. I would like to be thinner and I would especially like to have a flatter stomach/ thinner thighs/ smaller _____. But right now, this is what I weigh and this is the body I've got … and I am going to *accept* myself at that!"

Once you realize this level of self-acceptance, you are ready for the final "I do." in the marriage of your mind and body. But … while you have come this far, the last step may prove your most challenging! Again, let's look to Cindy for direction.

MORE REFLECTIONS ON DIETING

In The Game of Dieting, Cindy holds the trump card up her sleeve — *but* — ironically, she is unwilling to lay down her winning hand. Blinded by her unquestioning faith in diets, Cindy believes that the only "weigh" for her to succeed at weight loss is to continue playing the game. As a result, she ignores what her personal experiences decisively point to. In essence, Cindy is acutely aware of how her body reacts to dieting (so much so, she was able to beautifully relay her observations to me), but … *she remains paralyzed to act upon that knowledge!*

Thus, while I listened to Cindy on the bus that day, I could see that the road leading towards her dieting salvation is, in essence, a passageway towards self-acceptance that I had chosen, but she was not yet willing to journey. Instead, Cindy continues to circle endlessly on dieting routes that repeatedly take her nowhere — but fatter! She refuses to opt for the road less travelled, a road that will deliver her to a destination where diets do not exist.

Why?!

Why is it so difficult for Cindy and other chronic weight watchers to give up dieting?! I mean, why do we continue to pin our hopes on the belief that one day we will stumble upon a magical two week diet that will solve our weight problems for good?

Unfortunately, it is not that simple. Unfortunately, science has not yet developed a two week diet that, when followed once, will grant perpetual slimness and enable us to eat happily and thinly ever after!

But, Cindy will not accept this. Despite her continual frustration. Despite her perpetual disappointment. And despite the overwhelming evidence to the contrary (her repeated failures), Cindy *still* believes in dieting!

This was clearly evident following our discussion on the bus. For as we parted that day, Cindy turned to me and said, "*I think I'll 'go for it' on Monday. Yes, I'm ready to start another diet this Monday.*"

Can you believe it?!

Can you really believe that **Cindy was willing to go on yet another diet**!?!

I most surely could not. In fact, I just about keeled over on the spot!

And predictably, Cindy's conviction to start that diet many Monday mornings ago was thwarted, as it has been time and again since. For today she is fatter than she has ever been!

FOOD FOR THOUGHT

Sadly, Cindy has the answer to her weight problem at her fingertips, but her mind has yet to fully accept what her heart and soul already know.

AND THIS IS WHERE THE TRUE MARRIAGE OF MIND AND BODY HAS TO TAKE PLACE!

Somewhere along the way, the "aha" has to be experienced where the internal light bulb of illumination clicks on and understanding fuses with reality.

However, this can not happen if you are determined to cling desperately to dieting. Oh no. You must let go of that false security blanket and step over the threshold that Cindy refuses to cross. Cindy knows the truth in her mind, but she can not interface it upon her reality — yet. She does not want to acknowledge that the solution to her weight problem is *to eat and exercise moderately on a regular and permanent basis*.

FURTHER FOOD FOR THOUGHT

Now are you saying to yourself, "You mean I read this entire book just to be told to eat and exercise normally?"

Yes.

But if you really think about it, can't you see that *eating normally and exercising regularly constitute the ultimate answer*?

How can I be so sure?

Because I suffered *miserably* for years. And when I finally took a few steps back from the brink of dieting to assess my overall situation, I decided I could not (and would not!) walk the dieting tightrope any longer. My attitude towards food and weight was bordering on an obsession; and I was tired of balancing the emotional wear and tear! This fear and fatigue — heightened by the loss of my period — forced me to realize (Thank God!) that I had simply *had it*! with constantly worrying about food. In fact, the thought of spending the rest of my life enmeshed in dieting made my stomach turn and mind cringe!

I guess it is similar to a battered wife, or an alcoholic, or anyone whose life is dominated by a pervading negative force. One morning, based upon a culmination of everything, the abused wakes up and *finally* says, "*I've had it*! *I can't take this any longer, and I am going to do something about it.*"

One day, I literally came to the end of my dieting rope! I ("**sole**"-ution) became so mentally and physically exhausted from carrying the weight of the dieter's noose around my neck … and frightened as I felt it draw tighter and tighter, choking my very existence; that I had a mind-to-body talk with myself ("**soul**"-ution). And it was during this honest, private conversation that I embraced "**the ultimate solution!**"

I decided that *above all*, what I truly wanted was to eat and exercise like a normal human being. *Consequently, even though I was heavier than I wished to be at the time*, I said to myself:

1) "I am going to *accept* my physical being for what it is; and work in and around that to be the best I can be!

2) I am going to eat *normally* (*regardless* of where my weight falls!) by eating *everything* I enjoy in *moderate* portions!

3) I am going to exercise regularly *for the health of it!*

4) I am going to buy clothes that make me *feel* attractive for the weight I carry *today*, not for the weight I hope to be tomorrow!

5) I am going to live my life and enjoy my life *one day at a time*, and not be perpetually wishing I was thinner!"

This was the path I chose even though I did not know what lay ahead for me weightwise! And I have never looked back (or compulsively down at the scale) since!

Because along the way, I was able to formulate a more realistic and healthier perspective towards my body and food, which in turn provided me with the courage, strength and inner direction to overcome my abnormal eating behaviour!

Along the way, I learned that, ultimately, the road leading towards a peaceful and happy coexistence with food, begins and ends with *eating and exercising normally*.

 FOOD FOR THOUGHT

But again ... does this sound too simple, too trite perhaps to be of any value to you? Or does the thought make you squirm uneasily inside?

If so, **don't worry**! Those initial feelings of scepticism and discomfort are perfectly natural. For in your neverending quest to be thinner, you have conditioned yourself to believe that you *must diet*. You can honestly see no other alternative because ... *"How can you possibly stop dieting, when it takes all of the dieting you can stomach to keep your weight down*? I mean, you're already heavy enough as it is, aren't you! What would you look like, if you didn't diet?!"

Furthermore, for people caught up in dietitis, attempting to scale Mount Everest might appear easier than attempting to eat normally! You see, it is simply too hard to let go of that bewitching diet life line. It's like trying to break away from a poor relationship, when the rationale of "a bad love is better than no love at all" races persistently around and around in your mind. Unfortunately, the same unhealthy logic exists when it comes to dieting. "Any diet is better than no diet" insidiously infiltrates the life of someone who dislikes their body and desperately wants to change it!

But again, whenever you find yourself in that emotional space, you must ask yourself this.

> *If it were true — if any diet was better than no diet at all — wouldn't you be thinner (and happier) right now?!*

Thus, regardless of how disconcerting the prospect, you must shoulder the challenge and discard your dieting crutch! Once you make the break, you will be surprised to find that you can stand firmly on your own two feet; enabling you to take positive steps towards dealing effectively and normally with food. And besides, you can always retrieve your crutch and hobble on to the next diet whenever you wish. But first, give normal eating a chance. The physiological and psychological rewards are simply too powerful to ignore!

 FOOD FOR THOUGHT

But, what exactly is "normal" eating? What does it entail? And, how do you start to eat normally when you have conditioned yourself to eat otherwise?

Read on!

The next and final chapter will show you how.

Chapter 12

Ten Ways to Promote Normal Eating

Here are ten techniques that collectively will enable you to shake loose of the dieter's noose. Not only are these methods *normal*, but they are also physically and emotionally beneficial. Above all, they can be easily incorporated into your daily eating habits for the rest of your life!

(Note: **Each** of the following is so very important, that apart from reaching up from these pages and physically shaking you to ensure you comprehend their significance, I **can not** stress adamantly enough the major role each plays in promoting normal eating. So please, take them to heart and put them into action … with one condition. Do not expect to implement all of these behaviours overnight — just take one bite (and sip!) at a time towards eating more normally.)

1) DRINK WATER

I CAN NOT EMPHASIZE THIS POINT STRONGLY ENOUGH!!

Water is excellent for the body on numerous counts — but as far as decreasing food intake, its effectiveness is unparallelled! You see, water *naturally* curbs the appetite and restricts overeating because it fills up the stomach quickly, leaving less room for food and more room for you to feel fuller sooner.

With that in mind, *try* to drink:

a) As much water as possible — ideally eight glasses a day.

b) A mandatory glass (preferably two!) *before* each meal and snack. And,

c) One or two glasses when hungry (and *especially* when overcome by an uncontrollable urge to overeat!).

If you dislike water, drink what you can (particularly prior to eating). After all, some is better than none!

In addition, try spacing out your water consumption during the day to maximize the effect of feeling full without overeating. I find it best to drink a glass or two as soon as I get up in the morning and then continue from there. If I don't, I inevitably end up with the formidable task of having to swallow five or six cupfuls before I retire for the night. And when faced with that prospect, I usually opt out and head straight to bed instead!

2) SHED THE ALL-OR-NOTHING MENTALITY

Initially, this may be your biggest stumbling block. It was for me. You see, as diet junkies, we unwittingly condition ourselves to starve when we are on a diet, and to overeat when we are not. In essence, the *all-or-nothing mentality* becomes so deeply embedded into our dieting psyche that it completely dominates our relationship with food and makes it inexplicably difficult for us to eat like a normal human being! But persevere! *You can do it*!! … I did! (And I was addicted to dieting in the worst way!)

First, I'd like you to discard your dieting mind-set and all of the paraphernalia that goes along with it — including calorie counters, measuring cups, the bathroom scale, diet books and the oppressive restrictions of dictatorial eating regimes. Instead, I want you to employ a simple strategy. One that can be comfortably used at any time, in any setting. On Christmas day, at a Murder Mystery party, in the privacy of your own home.

I want you to …

3) ASK "THE QUESTION!"

Whenever you are about to eat, take a good look at what is on your plate and ask yourself,

"Is this normal?"

For example, *"Is this normal?"* ... A breakfast of one or two pieces of toast, with some butter or jam; an egg; and a glass of orange juice?

How about a *normal* lunch? A tuna fish sandwich with lettuce and mayonnaise on whole wheat bread; followed by an apple?

And how *normal* is that afternoon snack of a small fibre-filled bran muffin with a slice of cheddar?

That dinner of a BBQ Cheeseburger, coleslaw and some fries?

"Is this normal?!" ... **Of course!**

On the other hand, just envision a breakfast of fried eggs floating in grease, bacon drowning in fat, and pancakes swimming in syrup.

Followed by a heavy lunch of lasagna smothered in cheese, salad drenched in dressing, and garlic bread dripping with butter; plus two glasses of red wine and a large dish of Spumoni ice cream.

Then supper ... a huge turkey dinner with all the trimmings, including pumpkin pie heaped high with whipped cream.

Not to mention that midnight "snack" of a large bag of chips and a six pack of beer! ("What the heck!" you rationalize. "I've already blown my diet today. I'll start again tomorrow!")

"Is this normal?" ... **Of course not!!**

Is it normal to go rummaging through the kitchen raping every morsel of food in sight? ... *No!*

Is it normal to bake a batch of cookies and attack them before they've had a chance to cool? ... *No!!*

Is it normal to buy a dozen donuts and devour three or four on the way home? ... *No!!*

Normal to stand at the kitchen counter eating peanut butter straight out of the jar? ... *No!!*

Normal to starve all day and eat all night? *No! No!! ... A thousand times no!!!*

FOOD FOR THOUGHT

So what should we do when we know we are not eating normally? When we know we are constantly eating too much and/or inappropriately?

I know.

The solution is to ...

4) REDUCE AND SAVE

Believe me, you will be surprised at how easy and effective this approach can really be! Because *reducing* involves cutting down, *not out*! Which means you do not have to endure endless days and nights of tortuous stomach gnawing deprivation and isolation. Oh no. All you have to do to moderate your food intake so that you are eating more normal amounts is to cut back every so slightly by reaching for *one less* handful of peanuts, *one less* glass of wine, *one less* spoonful of potato salad, *one less* cookie, *one less* ...

Because small caloric *savings* are like compound interest — over time, a little ends up becoming a lot! And before you know it, your savings have grown appreciably along with your ability to eat more normally.

Furthermore, try to spend your calories wisely, by thinking before you eat and opting for nutritional food choices that maximize taste *and* calories. And in the process, remember this golden rule of thumb (or should I say stomach) — ***never, ever*** sacrifice calories for taste ... just have a little less!

Here are some specific examples of how to be calorie-wise and nutrition-smart. Keep in mind that these are meant as a guideline; not gospel! Everyone has individual preferences and tastes, so take yours into consideration.

WAYS TO SPEND YOUR CALORIES WISELY

If you are a tea or coffee drinker, why not cut back on the amount of sugar you have per cup? This will drastically reduce unnecessary calories in a relatively painless manner. Where I once had two heaping spoonfuls of sugar in each and every one of my umpteen cups of tea a day, I eventually cut back to none and now much prefer it that way!

The key word here is *eventually*. Because going cold turkey can be formidable and distasteful. Therefore, try cutting back ever so gradually (i.e. in the case of sugar, granule by granule if that's what it takes! It worked for me!).

Use "light" products (calorie and carbohydrate-reduced; unsweetened versus sweetened) when available and *tasteworthy*!

Don't refuse dessert (simply have a slightly smaller piece).

Choose fresh fruit over tinned; or fruit packed in natural juices rather than heavy syrup.

Spread your sandwich with either mayonnaise *or* butter. Or use light mayonnaise and lo-cal margarine — ***but only if the taste appeals to you***.

Have jam *or* butter on your toast. If you like both, use a little, not a lot of each.

Opt for a gin and *diet* tonic … a rum and *diet* Coke … a *lite* beer … a glass of wine versus a Mai Tai or Pina Colada.

Find a diet salad dressing (fat-free and/or calorie-reduced) that really tickles your taste buds!

Order a plain, grilled steak instead of one swamped under Béarnaise (or have the sauce served on the side).

Choose poached or boiled eggs as opposed to fried.

Don't have seconds — they are doubly fattening and rarely taste as good as firsts!

If you've had a big meal, eat a little less at your next.

Try leaving some food on your plate.

When eating, pause and ask yourself, *"Is this worth the calories?"* If not, don't finish it. Ditto, if you are full.

 FOOD FOR THOUGHT

As you can see, the possibilities of reducing and saving are end -"less!" And once you get the hang of it, you will find this technique unbelievably simple yet satiating.

Above all, it enables you to tackle the all-or-nothing mentality head on, while allowing you the pleasure of eating!

5) CURB BINGES

When overwhelmed by an unrelenting craving (remember Nancy and the "rape of the chocolate" incident?), **listen** to your body's talk and then respond in a dignified, rational manner. For example, when ambushed by an attack:

a) *Drink two glasses of water.*

b) Go to an eating establishment (a public setting will promote more civilized eating behaviour).

170

c) Order a single serving of whatever you crave.

d) ***Drink another glass or two of water*** while you wait. And then ...

e) Eat and *enjoy!*

If you still feel hungry afterwards, sip on water (or tea or coffee) until you feel full or in control. Believe me, one piece of Rocky Road Cheesecake enjoyed along with a beverage, will be far more gratifying and far less destructive than an all-out grab-anything-and-everything food bender! Physically your appetite will be satiated, while psychologically:

a) You are in control.

b) You are not denying yourself.

c) You are not feeling guilty about eating abnormally.

And above all ...

d) You are not vehemently vowing to begin *another* diet at the crack of dawn tomorrow!

 FOOD FOR THOUGHT

Everyone overeats at times — it's only natural. But when you do, don't dwell on it! Because that only intensifies the guilt. And the more guilt you feel, the more you'll eat! And when that happens, all hell breaks loose as far as you, your body and food are concerned!

6) EAT EVERYTHING

Don't feel like you have committed adultery if you have a Peanut Buster Parfait at the Dairy Queen, or Onion Rings at Burger King. These are ***not*** crimes! While the mainstay of your diet should be a selection of "clean" healthy foods (high in fibre, vitamins, and minerals; low in fat, sugar and so on) this should not preclude you from eating otherwise at times. Because your goal is to eat *everything* in *moderation* without guilt or recrimination.

The beauty of this eating strategy is that it normalizes your relationship with food while at the same time enabling you to satisfy your taste buds. And this adds up to a physical and psychological windfall that money can't buy!

Because *over time* it releases you from the compulsion to diet, and the compulsion to overeat follows suit — which naturally promotes weight loss and stabilization.

As Angie puts it, "I used to say to myself, 'If only I was thin, *then* I would eat normally.' But in order to become thinner, I had to discard that mind-set, and make a concerted effort to start eating normally right then and there. And when I did (as difficult as it was at first!), I found that eventually that panful of brownies and that jar of peanut butter cookies did not have the same power over me. Just knowing I could have some any time, seemed to scotch the compulsive need within me to go overboard! And it is such a wonderful feeling!"

ADDICTIVE FOODS

But what happens when a particular food does prove troublesome, even addictive? Well, when faced with this situation ... when you repeatedly find yourself unable to stop eating potato chips, for example, until you've devoured the entire the bag, you must recognize that you have a problem with that food. And over time, if you can not limit yourself to fewer chips; you may have to accept that, like an alcoholic, you have no control over your consumption, and as a last resort must practice total abstention.

I rarely advocate this, but sometimes there is no choice.

7) EAT SLOWER

Make a concerted effort to eat more slowly by taking smaller bites and thoroughly chewing your food. Not only does this aid digestion, but it also enables you to better taste and appreciate what you are eating. And equally as important ... eating slowly increases the likelihood you will feel fuller sooner and be less tempted to reach for more!

8) DON'T EAT WHILE STANDING UP

Whenever you are standing and eating, emotionally grab a hold of yourself and say, *"Put some food on a plate, and go and sit down and eat!"*

Because eating while standing may seem innocuous at the time, but it leads to the consumption of copious amounts of unwanted and "invisible" calories. Furthermore, standing does not promote leisurely controlled eating which, in turn, maximizes your appreciation and enjoyment of food.

9) EXERCISE

Exercise "for the health of it" ... *moderately* on a *regular* basis (that's three times a week; twenty minutes minimum). And remember, the benefits of exercise are *cumulative*! Therefore, *every single step counts*!

10) GET RID OF YOUR SCALE

What good has weighing yourself ever done?! I mean, has it helped you become thin — permanently?!

Of course not!

In reality, giving this manic-depressive-anxiety-inducing machine the heave ho is like severing the umbilical cord between yourself and dieting. It will put you light years ahead in terms of bodily happiness. Try it. You've got nothing to lose, and everything to gain (literally, and not figuratively, so to speak!).

WHILE I CAN'T GUARANTEE THE BODY OF A PLAYBOY BUNNY!

If you put these ten techniques into action and start eating and exercising normally, one of three situations will occur.

1) You will lose weight and stabilize at a lower weight.

This is what happened to me. Once I made the decision to eat normally, I found that *after a period of time* (about eight months) I could eat whatever I wanted in regular portions and not gain weight. Perhaps my metabolism readjusted; or perhaps I actually consumed less when I wasn't starving and binging. Whatever the reason, I lost weight, stabilized, and now eat what I want *in moderation*!

Moreover when I do feel my clothes become a little snug (after the Christmas holidays, for example), I don't panic and run for the bathroom scales, groping frantically for the latest diet. I simply make a concerted effort to follow the ten techniques more closely ... paying particular attention to drinking more water (especially before meals and when hungry) and cutting down *a little* on my food intake — just like my sister-in-law Anne!

2) You will stabilize at your current weight.

If that's the case, ask yourself this.

If you are going to weigh the same whether you diet or not, why diet? At least you will not be yo-yoing up and down physically and emotionally as you peck idiotically from from one desperate kernel of promised slimness to another.

3) You will gain weight and stabilize at a higher weight.

If this happens, I strongly urge you to continue eating *everything* in *moderate portions* for an additional length of time — another three months, for example.

Now I realize this requires a phenomenal amount of patience and determination. But … the dieting mentality may have sunk its hooks so deeply into your psyche, that it will take longer for you to completely extricate yourself from it and fully implement normal eating practices. Or, your dieted metabolism may have become so ultraefficient, that it needs even more time to relinquish its starvation protection stronghold. If so, I'm hoping that once your body realizes that *the famine (and threat thereof) is really **and truly** over*, your metabolic rate will readjust and you will lose weight and gradually be able to eat more without gaining.

But, what if you do eat normally and still find yourself heavier than you want to be?

Well, unfortunately, you might have to accept that you may never be much slimmer — let alone as slim as you wish! — if your body (vis-à-vis its metabolism and genetic stamp) so dictates! This is a daunting and scary prospect given your inner desire to be thinner. For there will always be a shiny new diet shimmering mirage-like on the horizon, tantalizing you with seductive promises of slenderness! And each will bring with it the provocative possibility of permanent thinness! ***But*** … you have to resist the urge, however powerful, to succumb. You can not allow yourself to be sucked into the allure of future diets, because the chances of their permanent success are *slim* and ***none***!

Thus, when temptation knocks (which it will!), you must repeatedly remind yourself of this.

If dieting worked, you'd be thin right now, wouldn't you?

JUMPING OFF THE DIETING BANDWAGON

While we have no way of knowing where your weight will naturally fall when you stop dieting and start eating normally, one thing is for certain! Regardless of whether you lose, maintain, or gain, you are much better off physically and emotionally to jump clear of the dieting bandwagon. Because chances are you will never possess the "perfect" figure, regardless of how hard you diet and exercise, ***but*** ... your body will settle solidly at the weight genetically predetermined for you.

And therein lies the significance!! ... Emotional peace of mind and body.

In the long run, it is best if you can accept yourself and your imperfections and learn to eat normally — putting the stress and strain of dieting and its incessant, useless worry and guilt behind you! The end result will be a more enjoyable relationship between yourself and food, and a happier, healthier and more fulfilling life!

 FINAL FOOD FOR THOUGHT

In the final analysis, the key to normalizing relations between your mind and body. The key to a successful union of the two. The key to unlocking the door of your imprisoning dieting demons and granting yourself the freedom to be the very best you can be, physically and emotionally, involves:

> *Assessing yourself for who you are!*
>
> *Changing what you can!*
>
> *Accepting what you can't!*
>
> *And then, eating and exercising normally!*

In doing so, you must realize that the key to your success is ***not*** another diet, another lost hope in the elusive weighting game. Just as there is no magical fountain of youth for those who wish to remain young; likewise, there is no miracle formula that will produce the quintessential body — regardless of how tempting different diet programs might be.

You must *accept* that!

And in the process, you must *accept* this.

Nine out of ten dieters **failed** yesterday. Nine out of ten dieters **will fail** today. And nine out of ten dieters **will fail** tomorrow, and tomorrow, and tomorrow.

Now, what does that tell you?

There has got to be a better way. THERE IS A BETTER WAY!

It lays within your hands and your heart!

The End of this book

… and the beginning of a healthier and happier you!

For additional copies of *I'm Dieting As Fast As I Can* please contact:

Pauline Dingle
2847 Mara Drive
Coquitlam, British Columbia
Canada V3C 5L3
(604) 945-9373